A PRACTICAL GUIDE

TO

GOLF PSYCHOLOGY

By Dean J. Symonds

Copyright © 2020 Dean J. Symonds

All rights reserved.

ISBN-13: 979-8-6974-9252-9

Dedicated to my family whose patience and support means more than they will ever know.

CONTENTS

Preface	1
Chapter 1: Self-Analysis	5
Chapter 2: Ability to Focus	17
Chapter 3: Emotions	33
Chapter 4: Self-Image	51
Chapter 5: Visualisation	67
Chapter 6: Confidence	79
Chapter 7: Strategy	93
Chapter 8: Preparation & Energy	113
Afterword: Being Practical	129

Preface

Information junkies. That is how our generation has been described. Do you consider yourself one? Maybe yes, maybe not, but it's clear that we live in an age of information. The last twenty or so years has given almost everyone on the planet the chance to seek anything on any topic. Sports psychology, and more specific, golf psychology has become saturated with new ideas, studies and statistics.

I believe the person who is reading this book wants to know; How does all that apply to me? And what can I do about it?

Now I am not saying that academics do not have good intentions, but academics spend the best part of their life mostly writing for other academics. So, when it's time to translate what they know to something meaningful and practical, there is likely slippage in what the public receives.

Myself, being on the front line as a PGA professional golf coach for many years, has had the chance to see what works in the real world. Away from theories, statistics and models, of which the scientific community is largely based. Deep down you want to know how all of this unquestionably great work, is going to help ME.

There are great pieces of work out there, from golf specific literature to general wellbeing. From the depths of Neural Linguistic Programming, the ancient Yoga Sutras to the many modern-day self-help books. My job has been to filter them for you, so you don't have to. You're not going to find any world changing revelations or "secrets" within these pages. If it's one all powerful, golf game defining "secret" that you are seeking, I suggest you put this book down immediately.

However, if it is practical tools that you are after, stick around. No secret is going to make you eat the proverbial elephant in one sitting. If you want to eat the elephant it has to be one bite at a time, and unless you have a huge appetite, probably multiple sittings. This book will describe to you how to hold your fork and where to direct it so that the fork coincides with your mouth. It will not explain in depth the complicated muscle functions in order to chew and definitely not the intricacies of the digestive system. I promise you that, if at any point we have to delve into theory, it will be explained in the most simplistic of ways. Others work will be referenced where possible, so if you are interested in the science behind it, you are welcome to investigate further.

I wanted to create a book for the reader which followed a very simple process. Firstly, introduce a system of self-analysis which can be done quickly and efficiently. No laying on the doctor's couch, no hypnosis, but something which encapsulates the whole dynamic between physical and mental states. Basically, asking the question: How good am I at this? How good am I at that? And overall; What can I expect from my performance on the golf course? The same way that a CEO of a corporation would study their organisation, its strengths and weaknesses and strive to improve for the future. But, like I said, we'll simplify the process.

Secondly, the meat and potatoes of the book will explore various areas and themes within the realm of golf psychology. Easy to find chapters on each subject will make it easy to find the area most important to you. So, in short, you'll be able to identify areas which are holding your improvement in the game of golf back, develop some understanding about that subject and most importantly, have practical tools to do something about it. There are thirty actual exercises and methods inside these pages, relating to different areas of golf psychology. Some are timeless classics; others are rather original. You will find some that resonate with you and enjoy them, others you may dismiss. That's fine, they are tools to be used at your discretion.

Although this book can be read in the style of a novel, I recommend using it as it was designed. That is, a practical guide to golf psychology. Start in chapter 1, gain an understanding of yourself, then move first to the chapters that are most important to you. You can always come back and visit the other chapters later. Nobody is perfect. Even the Ben Hogan, Jack Nicklaus and Tiger Woods of this world. The commonality that all greats of their field have is that they understand better than anyone their strengths and weaknesses. As a result, they work extra hard on their weaknesses. As a golf coach, I usually see the opposite. It's human nature to do more of what you are good at and less of what you are not good at. There are places where this might be okay. We all specialise in a job. I know vastly more about golf than I do cricket. But if your objective is to improve at one skill, for example; playing golf, we have to look at all of the micro-skills that are involved. Especially anything that is holding you and your enjoyment of the game back.

During an interesting documentary with Tiger Woods, in his own words he described what made him the dominant player in the world for two decades. He explains: Was I the best driver of the golf ball? No. Was I the best iron player? No. Did I have the best short game? No. Was I the best putter? No. The longest? The most greens in regulation? Best bunker player? No to everything. You see, he wasn't a specialist in any one part of the game. He was just good enough in each area, always striving to be a little better. However, there was one area where he was definitely ahead of the rest. This was his mind. And even here he still had weaknesses. What makes golf such an amazing sport is it will find and expose the weakest points of any that attempts to play it. Golf is the ultimate equaliser. It doesn't matter if you are the big boss, the wealthiest, the fittest. You can still top it in the water on the first tee and complain, blame something else and act like a spoilt child.

That is why many great players have stated that golf is more mental than physical. Some even giving it a 90%/10% ratio. Without further delay, it's time to start exploring your inner-self, your tendencies and habits. Let's chip away at those parts of your golf that are the most important. Let's have something productive to do next time you are practicing or playing. Let's enjoy this beautiful game a little more.

DEAN J. SYMONDS

A PRACTICAL GUIDE TO GOLF PSYCHOLOGY

Chapter 1: Self-Analysis

"The ultimate authority must always rest with the individual's own reason and critical analysis" - the Dalai Lama

INTRODUCTION

It should be difficult to open a book with content asking you to criticise yourself, however it is the greatest asset anyone can have if done correctly. The best of the best in all walks of life talk of failure being their most successful teacher. Getting up, brushing yourself off and trying again are the inspirational words of many that we look up to.

However, we are taught throughout life that failure is bad. The school system installs this into our minds at a very early age and then the concept is reinforced throughout our working lives. Yet many talk of their obstacles, and in some cases ruin, which contributed to their achievements. It was the process of growth, which is natural, that allows them to keep improving.

SELF-CRITICISING VS SELF-ANALYSIS

There is a correct way and an erroneous way of self-analysis. Self-criticising, for example; is the incorrect way. Self-criticising usually happens at the wrong place, the wrong time and in the wrong mental state.

Self-criticising in the moment of action is not the time nor place. This can be translated to self-doubting, which we will explore in a later chapter. But, when all is said and done, taking a step back and asking yourself some tough questions is a mature thing to do.

Self-criticising through emotion is never a good idea. Telling yourself you are bad at this and useless at that whilst in a state of high emotion can be detrimental. The simple reason for this is that your mind remembers information much clearer when it is associated with a strong emotion. Though this is a double-edged sword and can work wonders for positive thoughts, many make the mistake of recording vivid negative memories whilst in negative emotions. If you are of a certain age, I ask the question: Where were you and who were you with on the morning of 11th September 2001? Everybody remembers clearly what they were doing during this moment of history. I was with two representatives from a Dutch travel company in a hotel reception in Torremolinos, Spain. We sat there and watched the World Trade Centre collapse on a big screen TV in their lobby bar, terrified for the people that were caught amongst the action. Of course, emotions were ridiculously high. Fear, anxiety, anger, to mention a few, wondering whether this was the start of World War Three. Ok, try this one. Where were you and who were you with on the morning of 11th October 2001? If nothing evoking high emotions happened that day, I'm sure like me, you haven't got a clue. On a positive side, I bet you can remember vividly the day of your wedding or the birth of a child. Emotions play a huge part in what memories are stored and how well you can remember them.

Self-criticising and doing nothing is without doubt the worst thing anyone can do. What is the point of self-criticising if you do not take any action on the findings? How many times have you heard the following conversations in the bar after a round? "I couldn't hit a fairway today." "God, my putting is atrocious." "If it wasn't for __blank__, I would have had a good round." We even make humour of it. "I would've been better off putting with my driver." And the classic; "I played army golf, left, right, left, right." This behaviour is effectively self-critical and simultaneously broadcasting it to the public, which reinforces it even more. Worse still, no decisive action is taken upon it, so it's left to embed itself further into your subconscious.

Notice the difference next time you're watching golf on TV and the broadcaster interviews a player after a round. The player will mostly talk about good points from their game. The interviewer will rarely bring up bad points and if they do the player will not dwell on them and merely state they're off to the practice ground to "iron out" a thing or two before tomorrow. They re-frame the situation into something positive they are going to do.

So, how do we self-criticise correctly? Just flip the above three points around and we have what I like to call self-reflection. Wait until after the round, when you are alone, when emotions are stable and make a plan about how you are going to improve that of which you were not happy about. Ultimately, as the Dalai Lama ingeniously states, the responsibility is yours and non-others'. As a coach, the beginning stages of any session require identification of what the customer wants. You cannot believe the amount of people that don't even know why they are there. Spending good money and time and having no plan. Maybe one can argue that is the reason they are there, because they are lost. I argue, although not everyone will have the knowledge and tools to improve, after all that is the underlying reason we need teachers, everyone is capable of analysing themselves and having a good idea of where to start. Whether it is a technical, physical or mental issue. I really appreciate students who come to a session prepared with "I need you to look at this," or "there's always a time, on a particular hole, where this happens. Why do you think that is?"

Timothy Gallwey in his famed series of books *The Inner Game* applies a large amount of time investigating what he calls *The Law of Awareness*. The law is simple; *if you want to change something, first increase your awareness of the way it is*. Therefore, he continues, whatever increases awareness of what is will promote learning. It completely makes sense when you think about it. How can we change something if we don't recognise what needs to be changed?

In order to analyse and make a plan you need to be very clear about what it is that needs improvement. Let's break it down and obtain a clearer picture of your skill at playing golf using a technique I have developed over many years. The technique combines both the

THE TWO TOWERS OF PERFORMANCE

physical and psychological elements of what results in your performance on the golf course.

The Two Towers of Performance is a simplification of how psychological factors, i.e.; your mental skills, affect your physical skills. It looks like this:

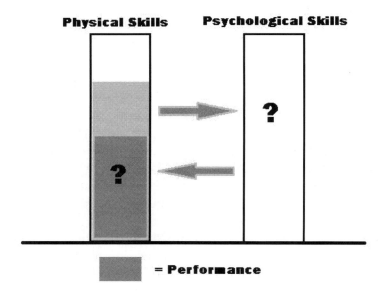

The formula is as follows; the application of your physical skills is dependent on application of your psychological skills. Each tower represents 100% and if your physical ability (explained below) is 75% perfect, how much of that 75% you'll see in performance depends on how much you have in your psychological tower. Therefore, if your mental skills are only at half their potential, you'll only see half of that 75% result in your performance.

This gives us a way of creating expectations. Although it can be argued that you should play without expectations, and that is correct. (A theme that we will explore later.) It is justifiable to have realistic expectations when it comes to self-analysis. It's important to remember that no one is perfect. Even the top players in the world who may have a physical ability of 9 or 10. They have days where their mental state is high and almost never miss a target. But on other days they don't play well. Has their physical state changed? Unlikely. What has changed is their mental state. Maybe it dropped 40% resulting in six out of 10 shots hitting their intended target instead.

The key here is to understand the elements that consist of the psychological tower and be able to recognise when one has fallen. Followed by something practical that you can do to heighten it once again.

THE PHYSICAL TOWER

Instruction on the physical tower is not within the scope of this book but we must understand it for you to calculate a realistic expectation of your performance. It is made up of everything in the material world that affects your quality of play. We always start on this side and we give it a rating. On a scale of 1 to 10, I would like you to rate the following physical elements that determine your input into the tower:

Physical Repetitions: How much do you practice and play? A quick look at the leading professional tours can show that besides a few fundamentals, your swing can be unique. It definitely does not have to be technically correct or a text book swing in order to play well. Jim Furyk, John Daly and Bubba Watson are living proof of this. Repetitions can be judged the following way: If you practice a micro-skill (chipping, short putts, etc.) every day you can justify writing down a 10. If you have never practiced and only experience these micro-skills whilst you are playing a competition write down a 1. Repetitions are accumulative. For example; all repetitions over time count. A complete beginner would be a zero. A rating of 5 would be someone who practices once in a while.

Quality of Fundamentals: This contradicts a little the previous point. However, even the worst of swings on the professional tours have certain fundamentals. Set up position, weight transfer, swing plane and impact position to name a few are very important ingredients in a good technique. Similar to baking a cake, if we use bad ingredients, it will still result in a cake. It just won't taste very nice. The reason for good fundamentals is that they produce consistency in the swing. We are not robots. For human beings to repeat a complicated movement such as hitting a golf ball with a bit of metal on a long stick, it needs to be as simple as possible. If your grip doesn't allow your hands to work efficiently and naturally or your body can't move properly because of bad posture, this is making a complicated action even more complicated. If you have a good understanding of your own swing you may be able to answer this one yourself. If not, maybe it's best to seek your local pro and have a swing analysis. For example; Rory McIlroy, Tiger Woods and most top players have very good fundamentals. They could rate themselves a 9 or 10 easily. Most amateur mid-to-high handicaps are lacking many.

Golf Fitness: I state Golf fitness and not general fitness for a reason. Many shapes and sizes play golf to a high standard. Many shapes and sizes hit a golf ball a long distance. Despite their weight or height, their muscles are trained to do two important things. Firstly, their muscles hold their body in a consistent and stable posture throughout the movement. Secondly, their muscles stretch and contract rapidly to generate speed and force. In some cases, this goes hand in hand with the fundamentals above. Some players do not use the full potential of their fitness because of flaws in their technique. However, some are limited by their fitness. It may be something that you can improve, it may be something that you have no control over. I remember teaching an elderly gentleman many years ago who had been in a motorcycle accident when he was younger. He could not rotate his right shoulder backwards. When asked to simply raise his arms in front of him until they moved above the head, he couldn't get past his nose. So, we had to address how was this man going to maintain the correct plane of swing if he couldn't move his hand behind him? Needless to say, it was an unorthodox solution we reached that allowed him to fulfil his potential. Health is not a factor. Where it does pay to be healthy in life, I am not disputing that fact, and your overall wellbeing has an impact, it is not essential. Many top players are not the best example of health. Some even played their best golf with alcohol in their system. I remember watching the legend and Ryder Cup hero Sam Torrance in a European tour event, he lit up a cigarette after almost every tee shot. He still played a great round. If you are someone who does golf specific fitness at least three times per week with no prohibiting issues affecting your swing, you can rate yourself up the top end of the scale.

Equipment: We can't leave this important factor out of the equation. Just like the fundamentals, we want to make a complicated action as simple as possible. This will be difficult if the equipment you are using is wrong. It can be wrong in two ways: Firstly, if it's out of date. This doesn't mean you have to update your clubs every season. However, technology expands into the gaps created by the rules. Sometimes technology expands so fast that the rules cannot keep up. We saw this during the early 2000's when manufacturers were utilising the spring of the driver face to increase the amount of energy imparted on the ball. Rules soon came in to trim this back a little. So, having modern, up-to-date clubs gives you an advantage, of course, to the sacrifice of your bank account. Secondly, equipment that is not correctly set up for you. Having the correct shaft, length and lie is vitally important. If it is wrong, it requires more unnecessary calculations in an already complicated scenario. Think about your own equipment for a minute. Are any of these points holding you back? What would you rate your equipment on our scale of 1 to 10?

Once you have a rating for each of the above four elements, add them together and divide by four to get a number for your current physical skill. This can always be raised in the future by addressing and improving any one of the elements.

Psychological skills are all the factors which make up how much of that physical rating you are actually going to see manifest. Below I will give a brief outline of each one. Try to be honest with yourself and write down a score of 1 to 10 again in each category. Be as general as possible too. The ratings do move up and down depending on the day. We've all had times where we have felt invincible on the course, likewise we've had times of helplessness. Think of your performance over the last few months or more.

THE PSYCHOLOGICAL TOWER

Ability to focus / prone to distraction: Do you have unwavering focus when it comes to playing your shot? Many describe this as being in the zone. You hear nothing, see nothing but the target. Or are you distracted easily? Do you find your mind looking for something to blame before you've even played your shot? Is that dog barking in a nearby house going to be the reason you messed up?

Control of emotion / emotions run wild: Do you play a round of golf without getting emotional? You feel the same whether you make a birdie or a triple bogey. It's just another hole, you get on with the job at hand. Or do you get overly excited and sometimes even arrogant about good times, but get angry, disappointed and depressed over bad shots? A bad shot or a wasted hole makes your blood boil that sometimes gets released in undesirable ways.

Self-Image as successful and deserving / self-image of a victim: Do you feel like you truly deserve everything good that happens to you? You believe it wasn't just luck, it was destiny, the universe repaying you for who you are and what you've done. Or do you feel like you always get the hard end of the bargain? Deep down you feel like you didn't deserve it anyway. You're generally not happy with yourself and keep telling yourself; if only...

Visualisation clear / visualisation, what's that? Do you have a good ability to visualise? You have a very clear picture and feeling of what you are going to do before a shot. Away from the course you, what can be referred to as day-dream, about all the good things that will happen. Or do you never use this technique? You can't be bothered or believe it's not necessary. You just throw caution to the wind and have little or no plan of a round or shot.

Confidence / self-doubt: Do you have confidence in your ability to play the shot that is required? You know you are capable; you've done it many times before during play or practice. You believe fully that you can lower your handicap or win a tournament. Or do you find yourself doubting your ability? You're not sure if you can play a particular shot, either through lack of experience or practice. You don't believe that you can play better or at the very least, not wholly convinced.

Strategy / reactionary: Closely linked with preparation, however strategy is the nuts and bolts that make up preparation. Do you understand shot dispersion and what it means to you? You understand the likely outcomes of each shot and plan contingencies for them. You play to your strengths and understand when to be humble. Or do you aim at every flag and the middle of every fairway? The terms and concepts above don't resonate with you. You don't understand the odds of a shot's success or failure.

Preparation / unprepared: On a macro level, do you feel prepared for the next round of golf? Do you know the golf course? Have you a game plan deciding where you want to hit each tee shot and with which club? Is there a certain process goal that you want to achieve that is not dependent on results? Or are you going in blind? You play competitions away from your local course with no practice round. You haven't thought much about how you'll play each hole to your strengths and weaknesses even at your local course.

On a micro level, do you have a solid pre-shot routine? You religiously follow the same steps before each shot. It's timed to perfection (not slow) and if something does distract you from completing it, you stop and start again. Or does your pre-shot routine change every time? Is it dependent on outside factors? You skip it if people are waiting behind or place more emphasis on it if suddenly there is perceived importance, maybe to win a hole or match.

Energy / tired: How high is your energy level? How important is it for you when you play golf? Do you feel sharp because this is the highlight of your day? Are you excited and slightly anxious because it means a lot to you to play your best and enjoy your round? Or do you arrive at the course in the last minute because you've had other business to take care of? You are usually stressed too much when it's time to start and wish there was more time. Maybe from work or maybe playing a competition with others causes excessive stress and anxiety. Or maybe you're just not that bothered at all, couldn't care less.

RATING YOURSELF

As we did with the physical tower, add together all of the results in this section and divide by the number of ratings, which should be eight if you rated each point. The number you have arrived at is how full your psychological tower is. You can see this as a percentage or simply a rating out of ten. Use the template towers in the appendix at the back of this book and draw a line or lightly shade the level representing how full each of your towers are. For example; somebody who rated an average of 5 in each tower would look like this:

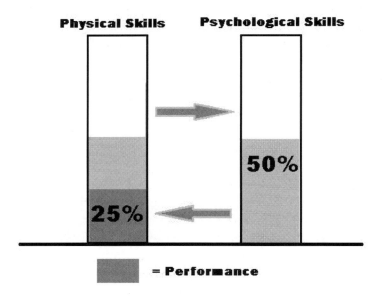

A rating of 5 (or 50% full) signifies that if this person was to have incredible, yogi like, Jedi mind force abilities and a rating of 10 in every psychological factor; they would still only be hitting the target five times out of ten. Their physical ability still needs development, either through more repetitions, better fundamentals, etc.

However, as the above example is only half full in the psychological tower, this will have an effect on how much we see in performance. You must lower the physical tower according to the percentage of the psychological tower. In this example the psychological tower is at 50%, meaning we will only see this percentage of the physical skills materialise. Our rating of five originally has now shrunk to 2.5 or 25%.

Performance on the golf course will therefore be two to three shots out of every ten that are successful.

Of course, the two towers model gives us the general picture and nothing more. Also, it is only an average. It doesn't necessarily mean you will hit 7.5 bad shots and 2.5 good shots every ten balls. You could quite easily play ten great shots in a row or ten bad ones. However, it helps to see a visual representation of what is likely to happen, especially when it comes to self-analysis.

We often fall into the trap of being perfectionists. Expecting that you shouldn't hit bad shots, particularly when you are improving. Our expectations grow during this period. It doesn't matter what level you are. Immediately after a period of good performance, maybe the lowering of a handicap or a series of tournament wins, this is the time when you are most vulnerable to perfectionism. There are many cases of professional golfers at the top of their game, who have won major championships, only to go back to the drawing board because they didn't feel like their skills were good enough. Resulting in many years of frustration and what is referred to as a slump.

I ask, was it really necessary to change your game so drastically if you've just won a major championship? Obviously, your skills, both physical and psychological were good enough to beat all of the best players in the world. They held up under pressure, they were put through the ultimate test, and they passed. Why the hell would you want to change them? Wouldn't you want to reinforce them? But no. There was this shot here or there which hooked and that could cost me next time. If I could only get rid of that by playing a fade instead...and suddenly they're on the spiral.

I've seen the same thing happen at the other end of the handicap spectrum on many occasions. Beginners to the game who hit a handful of great shots. It's understandable, and quite honestly a pleasure, to see their face light up with joy and admiration that they just made this little ball fly. But if we are not careful it can quickly lead to; why can't I do that every time? During beginner classes, if I had a Euro for every time I'm asked; what did I do wrong that time? Well, quite simply I'd be writing this book on a yacht. The person fails to see there are many little elements that goes into hitting a golf ball perfect. But for some reason, because they've learnt a few fundamentals and clocked up a few hours practice, that think they should be able to hit each ball perfect now. Ah, my friends, if only it was that easy.

By taking a step back and looking at the visual representation presented by the two towers model, we can see a clearer picture of what our expectations should be. We can forgive ourselves for those missed shots during a round and actually start to figure out why they happened in a thoughtful and constructive way.

After completing this exercise your job now is to review how well you scored in each of those twelve elements. Identify any that you think need improvement from the psychological tower. The remainder of this book will offer information in each area to help your understanding of the element and, more importantly, give you step by step instructions on how to improve it. If you've made it this far, congratulations, you are past the toughest part. Very few people like taking a deep honest look at themselves, especially if it reveals things they don't like. The beauty of doing this through a book is that you can keep it totally private. Only you know the conclusions you have come to, no one else. That is the truth about effective self-reflection and as the Dalai Lama told us; the ultimate responsibility is your own.

Chapter 2: Ability to Focus

"The successful warrior is the average man, with laser-like focus" - Bruce Lee.

INTRODUCTION

Ability to focus didn't find itself in chapter two by chance. It wasn't blind luck it was top of the list in the psychological factors either. The ability to focus one's mind is probably the most documented mental skill in all of history. It's otherwise known by a more common name; *concentration*.

Although, many do not like the sound of that word. It implies hard work, trying and struggle. Something you hear constantly from teacher to student; try to concentrate on this, try to concentrate on that. Mistakes happen when you lose your concentration, resulting in the phrase *"that's because you lost your concentration"*. Really, where did it go? No wonder we don't like the sound of it, it's like a constant game of cat and mouse.

If we look at it from a different angle, as in the ability to focus, it doesn't seem that bad. It's not a case anymore of mistakes happening when we've lost focus. Focus is something special that, when we get there, great things happen. To focus allows us to reach our realistic potential, it's an amazing place when you can find it.

OUR NATURAL MINDS

Our minds are naturally open most of the time. We are curious beings. You could argue that evolution has made us this way, we have five senses that are constantly on the lookout for danger. In the prehistoric times this was our survival mechanism. Our eyes and ears were there to warn us of something moving in the distance that could potentially be food for us or visa-versa. Our sense of smell and taste to protect us against anything poisonous and not edible. Psychologically our social standing depended on this and amongst a small tribe it was vitally important. If we were to make mistakes, we could easily be noticed in such a small community and would be shamed and fail to find a mate. Life was tough back then.

However, fast forward to the twenty-first century and society has changed a great deal. We don't live in a world where there is potential death around every corner (apart from certain parts of LA). Our food and drink have been cleaned and checked for us. Life is pretty comfortable, even to the point of being boring. But our minds are still looking out for danger. They are still jumping all over the place like monkeys from tree to tree. That's probably why the majority love watching conflict, disaster and despair on the television and evening news. It gives our jumping monkey minds a little bit of satisfaction when it catches something that is perceived as a threat.

Also, mistakes are far less important in this day. This is where ability to focus has been lost. When the prehistoric hunter was doing their job and had to focus, it was literally a life and death situation. If they failed, they could either be killed by the animal or at the very least, go back to camp empty handed and not be able to feed their family. In our modern-day world, we have created business, games and competitions as a supplement to these prehistoric practices. In games, which is what golf is, what is the worst that can happen? You might plonk a brand new Pro-V1 in the water. At the very worst, you might choke under the pressure of winning a match. But as Jean Van-de-Velde said after his famous Open Championship blow up at Carnoustie; "We're not doctors, nobody died." Credit is due to the man who, in front of millions, made the wrong decisions and looked like the clown of the circus, to really recognise the true minuscule scale of it all.

Therefore, our ability to focus like we once had to has definitely been compromised. Our readily distracted minds find it only too easy to be distracted nowadays, especially in the information overload era in which we are living. Minds are constantly being bombarded with stimuli, with the added bonus of whether it's correct, fake, propaganda, publicity and the list goes on. When do we ever get the time to *focus?*

Well the good news is; you do. It happens here or there, normally when you don't even notice or try to. Maybe you've just read the first two pages of this chapter without looking up, not thinking of anything else or being distracted. If you have, well done, you just achieved focus. During the last five or so minutes you were focusing on nothing else but my written words about some prehistoric baloney. We do use our ability to focus many times throughout the day. It's that moment when we are doing something and time just seems to melt away.

During my time playing and teaching golf I wanted to understand what caused this phenomenon and how we could replicate it. I found the answers in many forms. The Yoga Sutras describe the process of what it calls; enlightenment. To understand this, it is simplified very well by Dr. Ron Mann in his book *The Yoga of Golf*. The nature of the self looks like this:

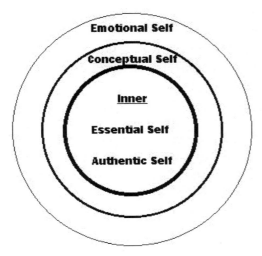

As anyone who has practiced yoga knows, the ultimate objective of yoga is to draw the senses and mind inward until you reach the inner

self. How does this look in golf terms? The emotional self is your reaction, your fear and expectations. It's the part that the world sees, the portion of you that is on display to everyone. The objective of the yoga postures and breathing is to bring those emotions under control.

That control is the conceptual self. This is the conscious mind continuously giving instructions. It is the thinking part of your brain. Also, the conceptual mind is responsible for the ego. It's always judging, either positively or negatively. This part of the self is unfortunately the one that is primed in our education. It focuses on knowing. It thinks it is the clever one, but it's not. I challenge you to take a golf swing and talk yourself through the action. Even if you slow the swing down, you won't be able to describe everything that is happening. The golf swing, like most actions we learn, is far too complex to put into words or instructions. In yoga, the objective of the breathing exercises is to give this conceptual self something to do, something that we can control.

Once we are totally focused internally and our mind is free from emotions, we can transfer into the inner self. It is the state where you are separate from body and thought. I know, it sounds slightly hippy or space-aged, but this is the state that all great athletes describe during moments of greatness. It's the process of just watching yourself without asserting any control or judgement. When we are totally focused on something we naturally move into this state. Everything becomes effortless. It is the autopilot, the all-knowing force inside of us. Science calls it the subconscious mind. It's the one that drives our car while we engage in a conversation with the passenger, only to realise we have arrived at the destination and can't remember how we got there.

THE PROCESS OF FOCUS

Another great explanation of the process of focus is given by Timothy Gallwey. He refers to focus as relaxed concentration, and states that *"control over one's attention is a fundamental freedom"*, however in this modern world it's amazing how little we possess. Concentration can't be forced anymore than you can force yourself to go to sleep, it only happens when we allow it. Hence, it has to be relaxed. He explains to achieve focus there are three stages you have to go through.

Discipline ⇒ Interest ⇒ Absorption

Discipline is the decision to do it, whether as a practice or during a moment of performance. I like to think of the mind as a lake with a waterfall flowing into it. When the water is crashing down causing ripples, any reflection looks distorted and unclear. By deciding to focus you are essentially cutting off the water supply (the information coming in) and therefore the surface of the lake becomes still and reflections are clearer to see.

The subject of focus must hold *interest* to you. This can be a direct interest (such as reading this book) or a perceived or implied interest for the future, such as the result of a great golf shot. If there is no interest you will find it hard to maintain focus and the mind will likely wander on to something more interesting. This is why later, when we practice focus, it is normally on something simple and boring. That's because if you can keep focused on something uninteresting, you'll find it much easier on something interesting or important.

Finally, *absorption* is when, as explained before, you lose yourself in what you are doing. This is the objective of all methods that improve focus. In this state, where your awareness is the observer, you are free from any thought. Fear, doubt and negative thoughts cannot exist in the present. All of these are future predictions based on a speculative mind frame. Here and now none of those exist. Timothy Gallwey states that he observed when his tennis students were playing bad, their minds were full of chatter. There was self-instruction, self-judgement and these were producing all sorts of feelings. Yet when they were playing well there was a quietness, a calmness, a sense of just doing. Does that sound familiar on the golf course?

Focus was top of the list because it encompasses so many of the other psychological skills. Taking control back of your mind is of vital importance if other factors such as controlling your emotions, self-image and visualisation is to be heightened. It's also extremely healthy and been demonstrated numerous times to have enormous benefits on one's life. So how do you improve or practice focus? Below we'll look at ways to do this on and off the golf course.

PRACTICAL FOCUS

We'll start with simple exercises that you can practice in the privacy and comfort of your own home. When it comes to translating these methods to the golf course it has to be very subtle. The idea is that nobody knows what we are really doing. I suspect it would raise a few eyelids if we were to sit in the locus position humming a mantra before each shot. So, it needs to be disguised into the normal actions that we would be taking during a round of golf anyway. However, for that to be effective we have to practice them away from the course initially. Here you can experience the sensation of bringing your focus into a laser-beam like Bruce Lee suggested. Think of it like sunlight, it's everywhere during the day and pretty harmless. Yet when we focus it with a magnifying glass it can produce a point so hot it can burn and start a fire.

I can tell you from personal experience, when you find that place, it makes you feel exposed and almost vulnerable. There is no protection anymore. The emotional and conceptual self are no longer there, their knowledge, instructions and lies can't rescue you. You have taken steps to trust your inner self, your inner actions, your inner knowledge and that can feel like jumping off a cliff.

So, let's start in the safe environment of your own home or somewhere similar where you can control the waterfall and cut off as much incoming information and distraction as possible. You don't have to do all of the following exercises. However, by trying each of them you will find one or two that you prefer. They all have the same two objectives: 1) to focus your mind on one thing and 2) to train yourself to notice once that focus moves to something else. And it will do. You might last seconds, especially initially, or you might make it through minutes. It's not really the case of; how long you can keep your focus, it's a case of how long it takes you to notice the distraction and bring it back again. If we were working a muscle in the gym you would hold the weight, move in a certain way so that the muscle took the load of that weight, then release it to a position where there was less strain. This is exactly the same exercise we are doing, but with your brain. You hold the focus, load the muscle, then when it releases and relaxes, you bring it back and load it again. That's one rep.

Many people through the years have told me they don't believe you can train your brain. "Oh, my mind is just far too active," and "you're probably born with talent and a winning mentality." I beg to differ. There are people amongst us who seem far superior such as Jack Nicklaus, Tiger Woods, etc. I'm certain they didn't get pushed out of the womb with a great swing and a champion mindset. What is far more likely is that they learnt these things at a very early age. Once learnt, it remained with them throughout the years. In fact, Tiger Woods specifically states this on many occasions. He talks of how when he was still just a child, his Father put him through military special force type training. It was kept more like a game, so he didn't realise he was doing it, but it was mind training at its greatest. He would challenge the young Tiger to play a round with him without being allowed to talk, all while his Father pulled out every dirty trick in the book. Dropping his bag mid-swing, walking through his line during putts, etc. But the young child was not allowed to respond, if he did, he would lose the game. Tiger states if looks could kill though, his Dad wouldn't have made it through his childhood years. Little did he know, he was being prepped for the massive emotional and psychological control needed as a champion golfer constantly on the world stage.

My point is, everything can be learned. Some have been fortunate enough to learn early, but you *can* teach an old dog new tricks. Here and now is usually the best place to start. Each of these exercises require only five to ten minutes initially, although you might enjoy them so much, you'll want to extend that time.

Exercise 1 - Counting Breaths

Start by sitting or lying down in a comfortable position. Place your attention on your breath. Don't try to control it, simply observe it. Keep your mouth open, however let air come in through the nose as you normally would. You can have your eyes open, however I find it is easier with them closed as there is less possibility of distraction. When you're ready, start counting each breath in the following way: Once the inhale breath has finished, mentally say to yourself; one. Once the exhale is finished, mentally say to yourself again; one. This is one round as such and we repeat the numbers twice as it requires more concentration to do so. It's too easy and too automatic to count simply in order. At the end of the next inhale it's two. The same at the end of the exhale and so on.

Firstly, set yourself at target of getting to ten. You will find if your mind wonders into other thoughts for too long, you will lose count. Remember, there can be no margin. You have to mentally say the number exactly at the end of the inhale and exhale. Use the sensation of the air flowing past your lips or the rising and fall of your stomach to judge this. If you lose count or fail to assign the correct number at the right time, start again from the beginning. If you make it to ten, open your eyes, relax, let your mind drift for a short while, then start again but this time to fifteen.

Exercise 2 - Counting Backwards

Similar to the first exercise, however we are going to count backwards from one hundred in multiples of three. This is very simple math that most people should be able to do. We don't have to repeat the numbers as in the first one. So, on the finish of the inhale mentally say to yourself; 100. On the finish of the exhale; 97. On the finish of the next inhale; 94, and so on. You'll be surprised how much focus this takes to keep it in time with the breath. If you can make it all the way down to zero you have done fantastic. But, if you lose count or the timing of the breaths, start again from one hundred.

Exercise 3 - Clock Watching

This exercising is actually a little more interesting than the title suggests. It requires a little bit of preparation. You will need; an old-fashioned clock or wristwatch with a second's hand, a piece of paper and a pencil or pen. The challenge is to place the clock in front of you and keep watching the small seconds hand ticking away. When it reaches twelve, at the beginning of a new minute, start marking on the piece of paper precisely on every third tick. Just draw a small line or dash, it doesn't have to be tidy. In fact, you shouldn't be looking at it, you should be looking at the clock.

Set yourself a task of two minutes to start with. It's very easy to calculate, if you have kept the sequence consistent there should be twenty marks on your piece of paper for every minute you are doing the exercise. At the end of the two minutes count up the marks and see how you have done. If successful, you can increase the number of minutes the next time you do the exercise. Remember, you can only write down the mark on exactly the third second, there's no going back and recovering. Once a mark is missed it's gone forever.

Exercise 4 - Holding an Image

Exercise number four is personally my favourite because it can be done anywhere and easily translates to a technique we use on the golf course. It requires you to select an object preferably in your line and level of sight. The more simple the object the better. Stare at that object for a short while, pay attention especially to the details. Study its size, its colour, its shade and any noticeable features that it has. When you are satisfied you have all the information about this object, close your eyes. However, once your eyes are closed, hold that image as vividly as possible in your mind. Picture it still there as if you had never closed your eyes at all.

It helps me if I first close my eyes for just a second initially and do this two or three times consecutively, checking to see if the object is still there. Then, once the eyes are closed indefinitely, mentally reach out across the space and see that object from as close as possible. Similar to the other exercises, once you catch your mind wandering and lose the vivid picture of the object, open your eyes and start the process again. Do not try to regain the image without opening the eyes. The opening of the eyes is the signal that you have caught your mind straying off what you wanted it to do. Opening the eyes is essentially one rep of your mind gym workout.

What's great about this exercise is it can be performed just about anywhere you have a few spare minutes. Maybe sitting waiting at the dentist, in a queue or especially whilst travelling, as long as you are not the driver! Also, as we'll see later, it can be used very effectively on the golf course.

Exercise 5 - Relaxation

The technique used in yoga to relax the body is also a fantastic exercise in mental focus, after all, the objective of yoga is to internalise thought. It requires you to lay down, either on a bed or exercise mat. Make sure you are alone and free from distractions, although you can play some soft relaxing music or nature sounds if you like. Position your body by laying on your back with the legs slightly apart and the arms flat and slightly out from your hips. This is known as the corpse pose in yoga postures.

Focus on the breath for a brief moment and allow it to slow down by making long, deep inhales and exhales. When you are ready to start, on the inhale, slightly raise a leg, focus on the muscles and tense them as much as possible for a few seconds. You may find it easier to start at the tip and then travel up the limb. Next, on the exhale allow the leg to fall back down and imagine a wave of relaxation moving down the limb, this time finishing at the tip. Repeat with the other leg.

After the legs move on to each of the arms using the same method. Next, slightly raise the hips off the floor, tense the buttocks, abdominals and lower back. Let them fall to the floor with the exhale and relax that whole core area so that it feels like it sinks into the ground. Repeat with the chest and upper back by lifting the shoulder blades.

Finally do the same with the neck, head and face together by lifting, tensing and letting them relax.

Now that your body has experienced the difference between tension and relaxation it will be more the wiser and by focusing on particular areas one at a time it can tell if something is over tensed. During the next round, start again with the legs, although this time gently push down into the floor on the inhale. During the exhale allow it to relax and return back to its previous state. Repeat on each breath for each part of the body as we did before. By the end of this round your body with feel like it is almost floating. Whilst performing the exercise, try as always to keep the timing in synchronisation with your breathing. The whole exercise may have taken five to ten minutes and it leaves your body in a deep state of relaxation to the point where it may take a determined effort to convince yourself to get up. As an added bonus you can place, what is referred to as an anchor in NLP, during the moment of relaxation.

PAVLOVIAN CONDITIONING

Anchors were actually first demonstrated in the famous Pavlov experiment in the late nineteenth century. Known as classical conditioning, you probably remember studying this at school. Ivan Pavlov was a Russian physiologist that noted the response his dogs made before they were going to be fed.

He devised an experiment which would measure the amount of salivation produced in the dogs' mouth. As expected, when food was brought to them the salivation increased. However, he soon noticed that it wasn't the food itself, but anything associated with the food. Sight of the lab worker who would feed them, the sound of their footsteps and soon just the sound of a bell used to signify feeding time. The food and one can argue the lab worker, were unconditioned responses. Meaning it was a natural behaviour that the dog would salivate when it saw food, it was hard wired into the dog's genes. However, the sound of a bell had no effect on the dog initially. That changed once the bell was used to signify food. The mind of the dog had now been conditioned to respond physically to an external stimulus, in this case a sound. Watson later in 1917 coined the term classical conditioning which involves learning to associate an unconditioned stimulus that produces a behaviour (i.e. a reflex) with a new conditioned stimulus. Little did they know, they were laying the foundation for neural linguistic programming developed by *Richard Bandler and John Grinder* that followed almost a century later.

ANCHORS

An anchor is something that we use to associate ourselves to a feeling or response that we want, or in some cases don't want. In the example of exercise number five we can use the simple word *relax* to condition ourselves to respond by deeply relaxing.

Of course, this won't work if we simply tell ourselves to *relax*. We understand the word conceptually, we know the meaning of the word, but our bodies and muscles don't speak English or any other language for that matter. We need to associate it in the way that Pavlov did with the bell and his dogs.

Whilst performing the exercise, each time you exhale, once the wave of relaxation has finished and you are free of tension, say to yourself the word *relax*. You can use any other word you like, *calm, chill*, etc. The word doesn't matter, as long as you consistently use the same one. What does matter is the timing. It has to be after the exhale when all of the tension has gone from that part of the body. With time your mind will begin to associate a long exhale and the magic word with the feeling of your body during the exercise. Voila, whenever you notice you are starting to feel tense and anxious perform the anchor and your body will remember that lovely feeling of laying on your bed, relaxed and not a care in the world.

BRINGING FOCUS TO THE GOLF COURSE

So now we have experienced focus in the comfort of our own home, it's time to bring it out to the golf course, or at first to the practice range. Narrow focus is the ultimate goal of a good pre-shot routine which we will explore in that chapter. However, it can be and should be practiced throughout the round. As we now know, focus is the ability to control your thoughts, specifically from a wide-open mind to a narrow one. Think of it like a radio. If we could pick up all of the frequencies at once there would be a mess of music and chatter. When we use the dial to narrow down and filter what is received, we hear something clear and understandable.

In reality we need to do this constantly whilst playing golf. You can't always be on narrow focus, it requires too much energy to keep it there, as you know from the exercises. It is something I see always when bringing beginner golfers to the golf course. Firstly, they are over-excited, anxious and nervous of their first time putting to test everything learnt in the academy. There is maybe a sense of having to prove themselves worthy. Because of this their brain does not rest, their conceptual self is trying to remember everything they were taught, resulting in far too many instructions and judgments. This happens not only over the shot, but as soon as it is over, they start automatically trying to focus on the next. "What club am I going to need now?" comes the question as soon as we sit in the buggy. "I don't know," is my response, "let's wait until we get there." Needless to say, after about six holes of golf they are drained. It's normal for a beginner to go through this and it is precisely why the beginning stages of taking a student to the golf course are always short and sweet. Over two hours for most will destroy them and may install negative feelings about the game being too difficult.

Those of us who have played the game for many years have learnt to relax the mind in between shots. There is a fantastic saying in the surreal novel Golf In The Kingdom by Michael Murphy. *"Tis a shame, 'tis a rotten shame, for if ye can enjoy the walkin' ye can probably enjoy the other times in yer life when we're in between. And that's most o' the time; wouldn't ye say?"* I believe in this statement the mysterious pro with whom he plays, is referring to our ability to control our minds. You can either spend your time during the in between time thinking of the past and what could have been or in the future, worrying about what may happen.

If you can live in the present life seems much simpler and easier. That's not to say you shouldn't analyse when the time is right. Nor is it to say you shouldn't plan, again when the time is right. But we must let our minds relax between shots, enjoy this time, use it to converse with others and appreciate the beauty of nature which the golf course has in abundance.

We spend between three to sometimes five hours on the golf course during a typical game. Each swing takes approximately two seconds. That equals to roughly three minutes that we are physically performing an action. You can see now why some of the greatest golfer's state that golf is ninety percent mental. Okay, you say, but what about all the preparation that goes into making a shot too? Let's do the math. A pre-shot routine should take about twenty seconds maximum. That's a total of twenty-six minutes for a golfer who takes eighty shots. Let's just imagine that you spend one whole minute assessing your lie, the wind, distance, etc. before you make the shot. That's eighty minutes of golf, during a time of three to five hours on the course.

Therefore, the concept of wide and narrow focus is definitely an important one. It needs to be wide in between shots, but stay in the present. Then it must narrow when it is time to play. So how can we apply our newly learnt skill to focus during a game of golf? Firstly, we'll look at what you can do to control your mind during the *in between* moments.

Method 1 - Breathing whilst walking

For those of you who do not use buggies, synchronising your breathing to your walking is a great way to stay present during shots. Many great golfers have commented on using this technique such as Colin Montgomery. Although it contradicts the theory of having a wide field of focus during this period, it is a great way to counteract any negative thoughts that might enter your mind. Breathing has for a long time been linked to emotion, which we will discover in that chapter. Breathing in for a set number of steps and out for a set number of steps can not only help you stay in the present but control your mental state too. I suggest doing it as soon as you leave the teeing area for at least the first half of your journey to the ball. Once you start to approach your ball let your mind open again and take in all of the information it needs to assess your next shot.

Method 2 - Listening and observing

Similar to the above method, during your time between shots, use it to focus on the environment. Listen to the birds and sounds. See how many different ones you can notice. Or look at the flora. The golf course is an amazing expanse of nature with a vast variety of vegetation. There are many top golfers who know all of the different types of grasses, bushes and trees. They spend their time noticing these, maybe commenting it to their caddy or playing partners. They notice the cycle of each plant depending on the season and whether they are healthy or not.

Method 3 - Converse

Start a conversation either with your caddie or playing partners. For heaven's sake don't talk about the last shot. Talk about something you watched on television last night or a recent movie you liked. Keep it light and trivial though, stay away from politics and religion. I have found in the past when playing tournaments that starting a conversation with a fellow competitor you don't know is a great way to relax yourself. Simple fluff talk is all that is needed. Where are you from? What's your home course? Or, how did you travel here? That is plenty enough to initiate a little conversation as you walk down the fairway. Pay close attention to the answers, notice how they respond. It's true, some people don't like talking much on the course, they may feel intimidated or portray it as an act of gamesmanship. If you get a negative response, back off, they may not be ready for it. However, often it can lead to rapport with the person and a nice friendship. Most people genuinely appreciate the effort and helps them relax too. There's a time and place as always. I wouldn't recommend diving straight in as you leave the first tee. Wait until the round is underway and after a few holes start when there is a period of waiting or a long walk ahead.

These methods are great for the in between time, however how can we narrow our focus when we need it; just before a shot?

Method 4 - The Energy Breath

A technique that works well is what is referred to as the energy breath. This is where we combine the relaxing sensation of the breath, as in exercise 5 and the laser-like focus to move thought internally. Before a shot or during part of a pre-shot routine, close your eyes for a few seconds, place your attention at the bottom of your spine. As you inhale slowly, move your attention up the spine, through the neck, over the top of your head and to the forehead. Hold it there for a brief moment. With the exhale, trace your way back down your spine letting your shoulders relax and drop, letting your core and lower back relax too as your attention passes them. Now is a good time to throw in that magic word from exercise 5. In these five to ten seconds that it takes to complete you have successfully internalised thought, controlled any emotions and positioned yourself physically and mentally for a good golf shot.

A word of warning though. If you are going to use this technique, it must be integrated into your game in a way that doesn't disrupt the pace of play. Fellow players will soon get frustrated if it looks like you are going into a trance before every shot. The best time to use it is just before it is your turn to play, whilst you are waiting for someone else to play their shot or the group ahead to finish.

Method 5 - Holding the target

As in exercise 4, this is a great way to focus your mind on one object. What better object is there to focus on than the target? Forget about the bunkers, the lake or the out of bounds, which so happens to be highlighted beautifully by colourful stakes to entice your mind like a moth to a lamp. Instead, pick out that little patch of nice green grass, an area on the green or the flag and hole itself. Make this your object. Focus your attention on this target where your ball is going to finish. Before it is your turn to play or for a few seconds during your pre-shot routine, close your eyes and keep the image of this target in your mind. Only this time open your eyes before the mind starts to wander. Any technique that can place your attention on the desired outcome (i.e. the target) is well worth doing. Your body tends to follow where the mind leads it. If too much energy is directed towards a bad outcome it is likely to manifest in a bad outcome. As I stated before, the subconscious inner self is a very simple mechanism in its true essence. It doesn't understand positives and negatives or truth and lies. It takes everything in for what it is. I call this the blue pigs and Eiffel Tower syndrome. It's where you say to someone; "don't think of blue pigs and the Eiffel Tower," however, because your subconscious doesn't understand negatives, it will picture exactly that which it was told not to. *Don't think of the water, ignore the O.B., I'm not going to go in the bunker,* are all statements regularly thought on the golf course. They have good intentions, but ultimately, they need re-directing away from the negatives to something positive. By practicing this exercise, getting good at it and using it when needed on the course, you are directing the mind towards a positive outcome.

The next step up from simply holding the image in your mind, is to do it whilst you are performing an action. This is the pinnacle of focus, the true sense of being in the zone. It is the out-of-body experience that athletes talk about and the endgame for disciplines like yoga. In golf, like most other sports, it happens when we are simply watching ourselves do the action. Our subconscious inner-self is free to do whatever it wants, we have total trust in it, we just get out of the way. And we get out of the way by keeping our conceptual thinking self pre-occupied with something else, in this case the immediate outcome of the action. We've all had that experience, a putt or a chip that you could see so clearly was going to go in - and it does. It happens when we were totally absorbed in the target, there was no other option but the target. Maybe that was our

> prehistoric survival brain kicking in for a moment with the attitude of live and let die. When we are totally focused on the target or the immediate outcome during an action, I believe it activates that primal part of our makeup. We become the hunter once again. This topic and how to achieve it will be explored more in the Preparation chapter, but by holding the image of your target and outcome in your mind you are leading your physical self in the right direction.

CONCLUSION

As we approach the end of this chapter, I hope that you have a better understanding of what focus is. How it is someplace special that we can find to bring out as much of our potential as possible from tower number one. It's not a case anymore of beating yourself up because you lost *concentration*. Granted, long periods of sustained focus are difficult to achieve. Practitioners of yoga have been sitting in ashrams for thousands of years to try and develop that discipline. Fortunately, in golf we only require it for brief periods at a time. If we can control what we are thinking of then we are one step ahead of most others that play. As Bruce Lee explains, the great champions such as Palmer, Nicklaus, Sorenstam and Woods are still just average people - but with the ability to focus like a laser.

Chapter 3: Emotions

"Intellectuals solve problems, geniuses prevent them" - Albert Einstein

"Our emotional symptoms are precious sources of life and individuality" - Thomas More

INTRODUCTION

I chose the two quotes above because I believe they encapsulate my opinions on emotions perfectly. Firstly however, let's define what emotions are. Emotions are the surface or crust that surrounds the natural self. Looking similar to an onion, the inner self lays at the centre surrounded by the thinking conceptual self. The emotional self is the outer layer, the one that is visible to everyone. Humans have an uncanny ability to be able to detect emotions of others as if it is some sort of invisible energy force that is sent out as communication. They believe that is what a dog's sixth sense is, dogs seem to be much more attuned to this energy than humans are. Dogs are very family orientated animals and are constantly wanting your attention and consent. The fact that they can't talk may be a reason they rely so heavily on reading your other signals. If you don't believe me, try smiling and say in an upbeat voice horrible things to your dog, it'll still be wagging its tail perceiving them as friendly. You've probably heard of terms like *body language, behind the words* and *vibes*.

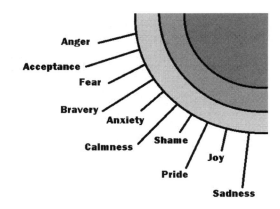

These are the unspoken words that are picked up during communication and give clues to what the person is feeling, not just what they are saying. The interesting thing is; not only are emotions communicating to others, they are also communicating to your subconscious inner-self.

TWO THEORIES OF EMOTIONS

As for the quotes, there are two main theories amongst psychologists regarding emotion. There is the belief that emotions are hardwired reactions that are triggered by a stimulus. These are the result of thousands of years of evolution. They are what kept our ancestors alive, they are why we have made it through time and emerged the dominant species. Therefore, there is not much we can do, an emotion that shows itself is our communication to the world of how we are really feeling deep down. As Thomas More stated five hundred years ago; they are *"emotional symptoms"* of life and define our individuality as people.

However, contrary to that thought are those that believe emotions are learnt. A young baby for example, has no reason to fear a flame until they are burnt or feel the heat. Throughout our lives we are conditioned to react a certain way in any given situation, depending on what we learn we all react in a different way. Some people jump off cliffs and buildings for entertainment whereas others would dread the thought of it. People find happiness and joy in different things, some cry at movies constantly, others have no reaction. Although Albert Einstein's quote was meant purely in terms of science, I believe it describes the mind of a great athlete perfectly. We know in sports that too much emotion can damage performance, all sports psychologists seem to agree on this fact. Therefore, if you can prevent the escalation then you have prevented the problem from arising rather than having to solve it. However, I get frustrated when reading that many psychologists in the top of their field essentially say play without emotion. They say you shouldn't play with fear, it doesn't exist on the golf course. You shouldn't get angry, you shouldn't get excited, just play one shot at a time and count them up at the end. It seems like a magical solution, just take emotions out of the picture and everything will be okay. Just delete that part of human nature off the hard-drive and you're set to go. Be like a machine, a robot. Just hit the golf ball in the hole. Words of wisdom, but through personal experience and what I see in top players, it is clearly not true.

All of the top players display emotion. Jon Rahm is renowned for his anger on the golf course but still emerged as one of the best young talents in the world today. Sergio Garcia has one of the best long-term career records in the history of the game, yet I remember all sorts of emotional outbursts by the young Spanish golfer. From iconic jumps of joy to throwing clubs in the water and once even taking his shoe off and kicking it away as if he was starting a game of rugby. I don't mean to single out anyone, in fact a look at the table of most weeks spent in the top ten of the world rankings shows it is littered with emotional golfers such as Greg Norman, Colin Montgomery and of course Tiger Woods.

So how is it that these golfers performed so well over such a long period of time? Why are there so many contradictions to the recommendations of top psychologists?

THE SLIDING SCALE

Emotions are not binary switches that are turned on and off. They are actually a sliding scale. All emotions have an opposite. For example; fear and bravery. They sit at each end of the scale and we are constantly sliding up and down this scale depending on the situation. I believe that both theories of psychology are correct. We can't suppress emotions and stop them from happening. They are natural responses to our situation. However, if we believe they are controllable we can recognise them and stop them from getting too powerful.

I don't believe that emotions can be categorised as positive and negative, they just need to be the right dosage. They can help or hinder a situation, depending on how you manage them. If we can start to view these emotions curiously, we can understand them and react in a way to stop them from having a detrimental effect on our performance.

The trick is keeping the scales balanced and recovering quickly once the scale starts to tip too much.

One of my favourite sayings in sports psychology is *"either you're a player or a spectator - you can't be both."* When you are a spectator you can let your emotions run wild. Television companies and commentary teams are paid to heighten this. They will edit, replay and hype up everything that is happening in the real world to increase the entertainment factor. Emotion sells. A movie or story that doesn't evoke emotions is normally regarded as poor writing. Yet one that evokes happiness, fear, sadness then joy is a masterpiece. However, if you are a player you cannot engage in this rollercoaster ride. You have to keep those emotions in check. They are going to happen; you can assure yourself you can't do anything about that. It has been quoted many times that *golf is a microcosm of life,* during a round you experience all of the trials and tribulations within a few hours. But if one end of the scale becomes too heavy it can lead to poor judgement, poor strategy and less than optimal physiology. None of those lead to good performance.

Let's look at the common emotions you can feel on the golf course and see how we can keep the scales balanced. There are many different emotions that we feel and some are linked to later chapters in this book. In this chapter we'll look at anger, fear and anxiety, emotions I see all too often on the golf course. In another chapter we'll explore guilt and pride.

TOO MUCH ANGER

If the anger side of the scale becomes too heavy it will have a poor effect on your immediate performance. We all know that too much anger is bad in any situation in life. Firstly, it leads to poor judgement and rash decisions, the kind we wouldn't normally make in other mental states. Jumping from the frying pan into the fire, as it is known, I believe we are all guilty of this on the golf course at some point. It's when we let the previous shot affect our next. A wayward drive followed by attempting an impossible shot through the trees that would only have a tiny success rate at the best of times. Or a ball left in the bunker followed by another hack at it with no pre-shot routine or plan.

Secondly, poor judgement leads to poor strategy and a loss of patience in general. During a poor round we can lose all sense of the plan, hit drivers off every tee and shoot for flags that aren't accessible. It's completely the opposite of common sense when you think about it. If you are playing poorly you obviously haven't got your "A game" with you today. Maybe it's just nature's way of correcting the averages established in *Tower 1* of your self-reflection. Maybe you're just finding it hard to focus and get into a good state of mind. Well then, why the *hell* would you want to try and play shots that are difficult at the best of times? Surely this is a better time than ever to stick to a plan or maybe adjust it to make it easier, not harder? Golf is about managing what it gives you on any particular day and you never know what that is going to be. If you did, it would spoil the fun of it and destroy the allure to the game which keeps us addicted.

Thirdly, too much anger affects you on a physiological level. It causes tension, especially in the small muscles which get effected first and results in a lowering of your fine motor skills which took so long to learn. The touch and control, the fine details of controlling the direction and speed of the clubhead are lost or at the very least, compromised. This is a serious problem in a sport that requires so much feel and control. In other sports a sudden rush of anger can temporarily help, giving the player a burst of speed or strength. However, golf doesn't permit such violence. Tension over a shot only has one outcome, an undesirable one.

I learnt this the hard way when I was just a junior golfer of about eleven years. Even in those days, the late 80's, thanks to Madonna maybe, we were living in a material world. Every time we walked into the local Pro-shop of our club in England, we would look for the next fashionable item to make us stand out from the other juniors. One day, there it was, an impeccable Wilson imitation tour bag. It was a thing of beauty, newly on display in the shop window, bright red and white in true Wilson colours. It wasn't a proper tour bag used by the professionals. It had been scaled down, it was fake leather, but for a young junior, who could probably camp inside one of its pockets if the weather turned, it was a dream. Birthday time came around and I became the luckiest and happiest junior golfer in the country, well, at least it felt that way. I named it Mr Wilson.

A few weeks later, after showing my latest pride and joy off to the rest of my peers, it was the junior club championships. I remember it vividly. It was the eleventh hole and it had been a disaster of a day. Three more putts on this green was enough to reach boiling point. I stomped over to my equipment by the side of the green with all the mannerisms of a stereotypical teenager hating my putter. "Stupid club," I cursed at it, "Your laughing at me, aren't you, well I'll show you, you little bugger," and slammed it into poor Mr Wilson. It went straight through the W. There I stood in amazement, putter still fine and laughing at me, whilst my pride and joy laid there like it was having its appendix removed.

The first thought that hit me after the anger subsequently receded was fear. My Dad was going to kill me. We weren't a well-off family, I never kept up with the Joneses as a kid, but my heart and soul went into convincing Dad that bag would make me a better player. Here I stood, Mr Wilson only a few weeks old and ripped by my stupid putter (not me obviously). How was I going to explain this? That was the only thought in my head for the remaining seven holes.

After much deliberation I came to the, seemingly, clever conclusion that I would play down the whole incident. I knew I couldn't lie; the evidence was there and impossible to hide. So, I would explain to my Father that I merely hit the bag lightly and maybe the bag was defective or something. It should be able to resist a putter slam surely, they don't test for those things at Wilson? Christ, they sponsored John McEnroe for heaven's sake, they must make their products anger durable.

As expected, Dad was waiting up at the eighteenth green to see how I was doing. The delicate moment was close at hand. I putted out and as I was walking off the green one of the other juniors had beaten me to it. Dad had noticed the gaping hole and asked what happened no doubt. Along I came with the look of an innocent puppy who had just devoured a cushion, thinking of how I could manage the situation. I decided, putter in hand, that I'd show him. "I didn't hit it hard," I said. "Look, it was just like this," as I lightly lowered the club towards Mr Wilson for the second time. It went straight through the S this time.

Now I stood there over a dissected Mr Wilson, right on the main pocket, feeling like a complete fool. Dad knew he didn't have to rub salt into the wounds, I was distraught enough. He simply told me you're playing with that bag for the next two years and that's that.

Maybe the bag was defective, that second blow shouldn't have caused a hole. But I couldn't be sure. Because I had let anger reach a point so strong, I had lost all sense of judgement. It quite obviously distracted me from the rest of the round and ruined what started out as a good day. That is the cost of letting anger get out of control. As a by-product of anger, it can later turn to self-criticising and self-pity, two thoughts that I definitely had of poor Mr Wilson. I'm sure we all have similar stories.

So, what causes anger? I believe the majority of it comes from having too many expectations. It starts out as frustration to not achieving what you think you should. We have to remember though, that golf is a game of averages. You have to ask yourself the question; Are you playing to play your best, or perfect? As we know from the self-analysis chapter, perfect is rarely possible, especially for any sustained period of time. Learning to temporarily accept what golf gives you is a master skill, but acceptance is just as dangerous because it sits on the other end of the scale.

TOO MUCH ACCEPTANCE

Acceptance is a praised quality in society. *Let It Be* sings four talented guys from Liverpool. The problem is, greatness is never preceded by acceptance. It's the refusal to accept that drives people on to new heights, looking for the unknown, creating the unexpected and breaking impossible records. If we just accept bad shots without a care in the world, we will never get the desire to improve. We have to be mad with a situation in order to change it.

Acceptance leads to laziness. It leads to a feeling of not being in control of your own destiny, which is a whole other philosophical debate. If somebody wants to improve, it's the refusal of acceptance that ignites the fire to do so. If not, we just continue as we are.

As you can see, we need a balance of this scale to really thrive. All great stories have a villain to invoke our anger, our sense of injustice. We naturally expect people to be good and kind, but when presented with a character who is bad and deceitful it gives us this emotion. No different to a bad shot, one you have practiced and believe you should successfully hit, only to turn out the opposite. It should make you mad, it should make you want to practice it more, improve its technique so that it doesn't happen next time. You should definitely not accept it. However, the anger that you feel shouldn't affect your next shot. In golf it has to be brought under control very quickly. This is where you accept you are not perfect, nobody is, make a mental note and then get on with the job at hand.

This is the primary reason why we see so many great players, whether it's Sergio Garcia in golf or John McEnroe in tennis, succeed in the field. They have an outburst, they let off steam as to say, then get right back to the next task with more determination than ever. I'm not advocating that you should smash your club, throw it in the lake or rugby kick your shoe into touch. The more the scale is tipped the harder it is to bring it back again. However, don't expect to not feel anger, or waste your time training yourself not to be. Instead, recognise it quickly, do what you have to do and recover. How? Let's have a look at some methods.

Method 1 - The Invisible Line

A technique used by many top players is having a zone where they are allowed to get angry. There is an invisible line painted on the floor a few yards in front of them, when it's crossed it is time to let go. Any shouting, club air whiffing or tantrums have to be carried out in this designated area. It is important that anything you do does not affect other players shots or damage the course in any way. That is a way to guarantee loss of respect from your playing partners. Damaging the course is effectively disrespecting every fellow competitor in the field. I once played a professional tournament with a player renowned for having spectacular outbreaks during the round. The competitive side of me likes to see someone else breaking apart, it's one less person I have to beat because they are beating themselves. However, the young pro who was the third person in our group wasn't as comfortable. "I feel like I need to have eyes in the back of my head as to not get hit by the flying clubs," he turned and said to me under his breath. He was genuinely scared for his safety.

Paint the line, say what you have to, let out a *damn it* or something stronger depending on the company, but once you cross that line it's back to work. It's time to accept that you can't do anything about it right now. Maybe you can in the future, but right now what's done is done. You need to go back to whatever focus exercise you do during your in between time and then start planning for the next shot. There should be no expectations about the next shot or next hole because we all know that it could quite easily be a great one.

Method 2 - The Long Exhale

There is plenty of research in the psychology community regarding the link between emotion and breathing. The rate and sequence of your breathing is affected by the emotion that you are feeling. Therefore, it can have a reverse effect. By changing the rate and sequence of your breath you can control your emotional state. A recent study of this by AA. Sarkar at MOJ Analytics of Physiology is one of many that shows studies into this correlation and how you can apply it. The report states that the physiology of the body is calmed when the exhale exceeds the inhale. This is great news for us golfers considering the bad effects for golf that anger has on the body.

By breathing out slowly and consistently for twice as long as the inhale it tricks our subconscious self that everything is fine. So, combining this with method 1 can be a great way to get yourself across the invisible line. When you feel like anger has started tipping the scale too much, and that's a tough call to make in the heat of the moment, take a few seconds to yourself and breathe. Count the inhale for two seconds and then breathe out the mouth steadily for four. Let the air flow, it's not a blow, that'll just make you more tense. Allow your jaw to relax and deflate those lungs gradually. The added bonus of this technique is it helps to focus you in the present once again. The past will soon be forgotten and now you are ready to cross the line and get back to playing and not being a spectator.

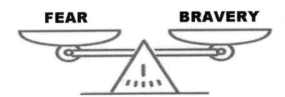

Fear unfortunately is one of the most basic emotions hardwired into your system. It's not going anywhere, but that's not to say it can't be dealt with. Fear is the predecessor of what caused our prehistoric ancestors to learn to focus so well. The effect on the body and the brain was such that it kept them alive most of the time.

TOO MUCH FEAR

Fear starts in the stomach causing it to churn and then spreads to the muscles making them tense. As it starts to build the heart beats faster, you start to sweat and breathing becomes more rapid and sometimes irregular as it tries to keep enough oxygen in circulation. When faced with a genuine threat such as a sabre-toothed tiger or a stampede of woolly mammoths it's a brilliant response system. Driving as much oxygenated blood into the muscles and focusing the mind on nothing but the danger is preparing us for the fight or flight scenario that is going to happen.

The problem is in the modern world we rarely have these dangers. In that case why do we experience fear at all? The human brain creates and understands any given situation based on perception, which in turn comes from information received. Unfortunately, information received gets filtered very easily, either by a third party or one's own filtering system. For example; somebody who is terrified of flying. You can tell them that statistically flying is much safer than travelling by any other means, that you have more chance of dying every time you sit in your own car. However, if the information that's being processed more is the fact they will be thirty thousand feet up, travelling at close to the speed of sound in a flimsy aluminium tube, good luck getting that person on a plane.

With golf the threat is always real. I've heard many psychologists say that it is only a perceived threat made up by the golfer. Whereas that is correct in the sense that your life is not threatened, there are other factors at play. We have a fear for our ego and our reputation. Nobody what's the reputation of a "choker" who loses their bottle every time under pressure. So, we fear the situation arising. We fear the last few holes when in contention to win however ridiculous that sounds to a non-golfer psychologist. Especially if we have had a bad experience previously. Someone who has thrown away a chance to win now has many other negative emotions associated with that experience and naturally will want to avoid it again in the future.

Another type of threat is fear of failure. In some cases, especially the professional golfer, failure could equal bankruptcy, poverty and maybe a feeling of wasted practice and all the time dedicated to it. World number one Greg Norman admits in his biography *The Way of the Shark*, this was his primary motivator. The fear of failing is what made him practice more than anyone else and drove him on to improve. The problem with fear of failure is it can easily turn into a fear of taking chances. Avoiding risk gives you a sense of staying in your comfort zone because any challenge would take you out of it.

Fear of success is the opposite and can be described more as a fear of the unknown. Plenty of times throughout history we have seen players win major championships only to disappear altogether afterwards. This is an all too common fear that can prevent somebody from wanting to reach the limelight and all of the expectations that come with it. I know it seems completely counter intuitive. Why would you be playing a game you don't want to win? But it does exist.

Basically, these fears all have one thing in common. They are either a fear of something known that we don't want to repeat or they are fear of the unknown. However, one thing is for sure; it's not a fear of any physical harm, which the emotion was designed for. Place me in a boxing ring with a hungry Mike Tyson and I would genuinely fear for my safety and the safety of my ears. Why? Because I've experienced physical pain before through contact sports and it's not enjoyable when you are hurt. Place me in the final group of the Masters alongside the best players in the world with millions watching throughout the world and I would feel fear. Why? Because I've never experienced that before. I'm not saying it wouldn't be an amazing experience, I'm sure it would, but it seems scary for someone who's only played in front of a few hundred at the most in small professional events. Thinking about a future event that would take you out of your comfort zone induces fear.

Both types of fear are justifiable. Although one is real present fear and the other is perceived fear. The good news is we can counteract fear with small steps of its opposite, which is called bravery.

TOO MUCH BRAVERY

Too much bravery can be just as detrimental as fear. Bravery is an emotion that is portrayed as heroic, macho and sometimes super-human. Life is not Hollywood though. There is a point when bravery becomes just plain stupidity. That soldier you see on the television screen, sword drawn and running alone into battle wouldn't last ten seconds in the real world. If he was more in touch with his fear, as to say the scales were a little more balanced, he would be running the other way and maybe get the chance to fight another day.

This happens on the golf course when the golfer tries to attempt things that have very little chance of success. It could be hitting a driver on a tight hole or firing at a flag surrounded by danger. It could be trying to carry a water hazard or miraculously escaping from trouble to the green. Too much bravery leads to poor judgement and poor strategy mostly. It often manifests when we are angry as an attempt of instant gratification. Kevin Costner represents this perfectly in the movie *Tin Cup*. Ultimately his brave, never lay-up, attitude is his downfall, although it all ends well, but let's not forget it's Hollywood.

There are moments to be brave, certainly. However, it shouldn't be at the expense of judgement. We could call it a calculated risk. There are also moments to be humble, realise your limitations and put the sword away. It's a choice that sooner or later every sportsperson has to make. The easy way to think about it is; how many times am I going to be successful? Exempt of extreme circumstances, if I am going to lose the gamble more times than I will win, then I am nothing more than a gambler. The underlying addiction to gambling is a desire to experience that dopamine produced from winning, no matter how many losses it takes.

Trying to play the miracle shot all of the time will produce a large number of disappointments compared to the minimal amount of times you get that chemical. Yes, in golf you generally only win a tiny amount of times compared to the tournaments you play, that is true. However, golf is the accumulation of all the shots and decisions you make, it's not based on one shot. The only time it is okay to gamble is if it does come down to one shot. Maybe in that sense Kevin should have gone for the green on the eighteenth, the first time anyway. After the third attempt he was just after the dopamine.

As always, we need a balance. Too much fear will paralyze you, too much bravery will mostly end in disappointment. We need to recognise fear. We need to recognise when a shot is too difficult and form a strategy to escape with the least amount of damage. Golf has been called a game of damage limitation. Avoid the obstacles and you are going to have an easier time on the course. However, we need a little bravery in order to progress and step out of our comfort zone. If not, we are unlikely to move forward. It takes a certain amount of bravery to recognise our weaknesses and ask someone for help. Let's look at how we can deal with these issues in golf.

Method 1 - Facing your fear

As unpopular as it may sound, facing your fear is a big step to overcoming it. This doesn't mean you should jump straight into the deep end of the pool not knowing how to swim. The correct way to do it is to first recognise what the fear is and how it makes you feel. Then break the challenge down into smaller steps. Simulate a lesser version of what makes you scared and become accustomed to that first. For example; somebody afraid of snakes is not going to wrap themselves in a boa-constrictor, but they might hold a worm. From here, once they become used to the wriggling sensation of a worm, they could hold a baby snake and realise that it's not that bad.

In a golf scenario top level golfers slowly become accustomed to spectators, cameramen and other distractions as they progress through the ranks. By slowly facing your fears you become desensitised to them and they don't overwhelm you. For beginner golfers, an initial fear may be playing with others or other people watching on the first tee. The first step is to play with friends or someone you are confident with. From there you could join with other strangers whilst still under the protection of your usual partner. After realising that the majority of other players are kind and encouraging (and are normally too self-occupied to be judging you) it could be time to sign up for a local competition and play with others outside of your circle.

It takes the same little slice of bravery each time you take a step towards your goal instead of a large chunk of bravery to do it all at once. That way we can keep the scales balanced.

Desensitising yourself slowly is a very strong strategy when facing a fear. Many years ago, when I was considering turning professional, I was terrible in bunkers. I had been a good junior raised in high level competition and carried on in the amateur ranks enjoying competing whenever I could. However, the sand was my Achilles heel. I had the fear that one day I would make a fool of myself, especially if there was a crowd watching. I realised there was no avoiding it, it was inevitable that one day I would find myself in a moment of extreme pressure and in a bunker. Something had to be done.

I started by practicing more in the bunker than I had ever wanted to before. Then, when playing by myself I would place a ball in the bunker on every hole and play the shot, regardless of whether it was a good shot or not. Just the fact of being in the bunker continuously soon made me realise it wasn't in fact that scary. Once I had this feeling, I could take the next step. The next step was playing with a friend and colleague from the club. The match would have one additional rule though, you were not allowed to win a hole unless you had been in a bunker. There we were aiming at greenside bunkers instead of the green, hoping that the ball would go in the sand. What an incredible change of mentality, it had completely flipped from what it was at the beginning. I was celebrating going in a bunker because it gave me the opportunity to recover and maybe win the hole. Nowadays I have no problem whatsoever. That doesn't mean I'm perfect, I still hit my fair share of bad shots, but I'm no longer scared. I love it when I'm practicing and people stop to watch, I see it as an opportunity to show off my skills instead of being afraid.

I believe fear presents an opportunity to grow. Just as great investors such as Warren Buffett seize opportunities when the rest of the market is fearful, you can look at fear as a challenge to expand as a person. However, it has to be smart and strategic. Buffett doesn't dive in head first and gamble, he analyses and takes small calculated risks to achieve his goal. Think about what generates excess fear for you on the golf course and take small invested steps to deal with it.

Method 2 - Avoid things that don't help

Because fear has such an effect on the physical body you can help yourself by not helping the signs of fear. Avoiding stimulants such as caffeine directly before a round reduces the rate at which your body starts to induce survival mode. It makes it easier to keep your heartbeat down and the small muscles relaxed. The half-life of caffeine is four to six hours, which means that one or two cups you had pre-round are there for the whole game.

Likewise, excess amounts of quick release carbohydrates (i.e. sugar) will not help either. After high amounts of sugar intake your body releases a chemical to moderate it which is usually overdone. This results soon after in a decrease of sugar in the bloodstream that can fool your body into a sense that something is wrong. That's the last thing you want if you are confronted with a threat. Your survival mode will kick in even faster.

During a round of golf make sure you are well hydrated. Consume sports drinks that contain moderate amounts of sugar. Stay away from Coca-Cola, Red Bull and other such energy drinks. Eat slow carbohydrates like nuts and cereals. If your body is happy it is less likely to display signs of fear when it arrives and you can think your way out of the problem.

Method 3 - Remind yourself you're Warren Buffett

Golf is a marathon not a sprint. Reckless acts of bravery can do as much damage as fear can. Actually, making poor strategic decisions too often can install bad memories and make you fear them in the future. If something doesn't feel right in your gut, your gut is often right. No matter what the ego is telling you.

Fear on the golf course is there to tell you something is not right. Take notice of it, it could be telling you to lay up and play smart. If you're standing there alone with your sword held high, it could be the moment to re-analyse the situation. Remember, it's all of the shots and decisions you make added together that determines whether you are successful or not.

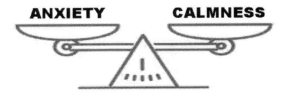

Anxiety is similar to fear in many ways. However, anxiety is the silent killer, always lurking in the background. Whereas fear is something real, anxiety is worrying about a potential threat in the future that might not be a threat at all. The problem is it invokes the same physical reactions as fear although milder, but constantly over a longer period of time.

TOO MUCH ANXIETY

This can be very bad for your health if it is not dealt with. Unfortunately, living with anxiety is ever more common in our society. We don't have the direct threat of fear much anymore, but the constant worrying over one's job, relationship, money, etc. is our new fear. The main problem is it doesn't pass like real fear does, it lingers and builds very slowly.

In golf, anxiety is usually connected to fear of the unknown. We truly do not know what to expect for a round of golf. It doesn't matter how much we've practiced, how good our strategy is, how high our confidence is. All these things improve our chances, but when the time comes to tee the ball up on the first hole, it's the golfing gods who decide whether you are going to get the luck or not. It's the golfing gods that will give you a good bounce or a bad bounce, a lip in or a lip out. All we can do is manage the situation to the best of our ability. That uncertainty produces anxiety. When we are confronted by the unknown, doubt can creep in and we naturally tense. However, like all the other emotions, it's normal to feel a certain degree of anxiety, but we have to keep the levels low. Anxiety only shows that you care about what is going to happen. Many top-level professionals have stated that even after decades of playing, they still get anxious on the first tee shot. They go on to say that when the day comes that they no longer have that feeling, it would be time to hang up the boots because it means playing competitively is not important to them anymore. Once the round starts it recedes, autopilot kicks in and the plan is put into action, but it's the build-up before the round commences where anxiety plays its part.

TOO MUCH CALMNESS

It sounds counter-productive to say too calm, but the theme of this book is to explore what *really* happens in golf, not just what psychological models say. Too much calmness can be translated to not caring at all. If the scale is tipped too far towards this extreme a player probably doesn't understand why they play golf. They have no interest in the outcome. It is stated often in sports literature that you should forget about the outcome and focus only on the process. This is correct; however, it is the means to an end. If you don't know what the end is you are essentially a captain without a map.

Every top athlete has goals and as soon as you have a goal anxiety has to be present because you don't know if you are going to achieve it or not. If calmness is at such an extreme that it becomes *carelessness*, a player's goals are not important anymore or don't even exist in the first place. I'm not saying don't be *calm,* of course you should, especially if you feel anxiety creeping up on you. Just don't throw all of your caution to the wind. Take your destiny into your own hands. Yes, the golfing gods will decide whether you get lucky today or whether those two putts that sat on the edge of the hole will cost you the match. However, we must have some direction, we can't leave it all up to them. Sit down, think about what you would like to achieve in the game, write it down and, as soon as you do, you will stop the scales from tipping too far into carelessness.

DEALING WITH ANXIETY

Step 1 - Identify Why

Realise it's okay to feel anxiety and try to identify exactly what it is that is causing you to feel this way. Is it a future tournament? Is it the thought of stepping outside your circle of friends and playing with strangers? Is it because you are worried you might not achieve your goal? When you start to feel those butterflies in your stomach, it's a good indicator that you have the underlying reason. Bring it out to the world, either by writing it down or talking sincerely with someone. This is an important step, there is a lot of power in writing a problem down and making it official. Once the problem is laid out in front of you, we can start to look at it logically.

Step 2 - Analyse it

Once the cause of the anxiety is written down in front of you, try to look at it like you would if you were a business owner. How far in the future is it? What are the outcomes it could produce, negative and positive? What would cause that to happen? The more you understand about the issue the more comfortable you will start to feel. Finally, the most important question is; is it something that I can control? If it isn't; what measures could I take to protect myself or limit its effect? More often than not on the golf course, the perceived threat is a mixture of both controllable and uncontrollable. You can do everything to the best of your ability and still get beaten by someone else who played better or had luck on their side that day. If you can plan contingencies ahead of time, suddenly the unknown becomes a little more known and levels of anxiety subside.

Step 3 - Stay in the Present

Any of the methods in chapter 2 will work great to counteract anxiety. If we understand that anxiety is caused by worrying about what's going to happen in the future, for things that are not directly under our control, then it would be best to stay here in the present. Here and now we can control our breathing, we can listen to the birds, we can have an element of control. A strong and solid pre-shot routine helps us achieve this which we will explore later. Anything that can bring us back to the present and restores the level of calmness needed to play optimal is worth engaging in.

CONCLUSION

In conclusion, we have to understand that emotions are part of who we are. Many have been installed in our genes through years of evolution, you can argue that others have been learnt or conditioned throughout our lives. Emotions will always form a part of our natural-self, so don't try to ignore them or suppress them from emerging. Golf is not poker; you are not giving anything away if you show a little emotion. In fact, showing emotion and then bringing it under control to use it to your advantage can show others that you are strong mentally.

On one hand the player who allows emotion to get out of control can display to his competitors that their performance is going to suffer. Carrying anger over to the next shot, fearing a situation or making brave but stupid decisions are contributing to a downward spiral of self-destruction. Their fellow competitors can just watch, sometimes with horror, sometimes with pleasure, at the time-bomb about to explode.

On the other hand though, the player who shows a little emotion and then displays the ability to control it, portrays themselves as mature and wise. For example; a player who displays anger on a particular shot to then go on and recover their mistake is displaying a powerful mindset. A player who is mad at themselves after a bad hole, who then goes on to birdie the next three is going to communicate to others; watch out, I'm mentally so tough that nothing is going to get in my way. This display of determination can be a scary opponent in a one verses one scenario.

Again, like most subjects on psychology, it is the person's responsibility to recognise when emotions begin to get too powerful and out of control. To say that any emotion is either positive or negative I think undermines what emotions are. Fear, anger, anxiety all have bad reputations but we do need them in a certain degree. They do have a reason to be there, if not they wouldn't exist. Nothing in the universe is useless, everything has its reason to be. We also need bravery, acceptance and calmness to keep the scales balanced. But too much of these can also be bad for performance. We need the scales balanced if we are to be optimal both psychologically and physically. When one emotion becomes a little too dominant, we should take Einstein's advice and prevent the problem from ever occurring.

Chapter 4: Self -Image

"The person we believe ourselves to be will always act in a manner consistent with our self-image" - Brian Tracy

INTRODUCTION

The topic of self-image is an enormous one in psychology. Many sub-categories merge together such as; self-concept, self-esteem, self-talk with very little agreement on how. However, the overall view is that they all have a part to play in who we believe we are. The nature of sports takes place in the public arena, whether it's with fellow players or in front of spectators, and thus puts you on display. Golf is for the most part, an individual sport, so one can argue that your self-image is exposed more than other team sports which offer a collective protection. In games such as football, rugby or hockey, somebody suffering from a low self-image is less likely to be noticed and can also feed off the success of his or her team to help elevate their own. Golf, on the other hand, is you and only you. Having a negative self-anything will be exploited, not by a competitor, but by the sport itself. Golf has a way of finding your weaknesses.

Your self-image is built as an accumulation of all the experiences and thoughts that get access to the inner-self or subconscious. I say "get access" because our conceptual self has a way of filtering based on how we perceive the information presented to us. Remember the inner-self can't distinguish between truth and lie, it simply soaks up the data that is fed to it. The self-image is fairly stable but not set in stone. Because it takes the accumulation of information during a lifetime to form a self-image, it will naturally take time and many repetitions to influence it. You can't just say to yourself "I'm not a choker anymore" and expect that to work. You have to convince your inner-self to believe it. To function optimally it helps if you hold yourself in high self-worth, otherwise known as self-esteem and have a good self-image. However, many people live their life with a less than optimal self-image; here are a few different types of self-images agreed among the psychological community.

COMMON TYPES OF SELF-IMAGE

Low Self-Image - Also commonly referred to as depression, this is a person who for some reason has developed an undesirable impression of themselves over a long period of time. Surprisingly enough, this is actually one of the easiest to fix. Its main cause is distortion of information (explored below) and normally a case of just realising the positives instead of the negatives. We all have good qualities, just as we all have bad qualities. The person with a low self-image is usually only focusing on the bad. Once their conceptual mind starts focusing on good qualities the subconscious receives that data instead. In a game like golf, this is largely influenced by self-talk and what we say to others. If we condemn ourselves by telling our inner-self we are useless at a certain thing enough times we will believe it. If we tell others we are just reinforcing that feeling even more.

Unstable Self-Image - Another type of dysfunctional self-image is one of instability. This is the person who defines their self-image depending on the performance, result or outside factors. We see this displayed in the real world by famous actors or celebrities who at one moment are bathing in glory and in the next moment are in a clinic for substance abuse or depression. Their self-image goes from one end of the scale being confident, successful and deserving, quickly moving to that of depressed, failure and self-loathing. Then just as suddenly reverses. Although this is generalised greatly to make an example for the sake of this paragraph, this type of personality will find a sport like golf a terrifying rollercoaster ride. This person's confidence can be displayed as arrogance and cockiness after a good shot or game, only to fall into insulting themselves after a poor one. As stated before, your true self-image should be very stable and long term, it never fluctuates over the short term. If you display both extremes of any matter related to self-image it may be the result of an unstable one.

Distorted Self-Image - They say many models male or female, don't like their looks. The image they see in the mirror isn't one of beauty but a distorted version of themselves based on many pre-conceived ideas. The conceptual self is essentially focusing their minds on the imperfections or aspects they don't like, so this is the information being processed. In golf we see this as someone who refers to themselves as "a slicer" or "a choker." They have convinced their inner-self this is who they are. When you identify yourself as a certain thing, positive or negative, you are putting yourself in that box, whether it is true or not. During coaching individuals it's clear to see that many people think their swings are awful. Then, when it is shown to them on video, they are pleasantly surprised. "Oh, I thought it was a lot worse than that," comes the response. They often state; "it felt like I was doing it much more severely." What it shows me is they have distorted the feeling that was *really* happening and presented that erroneous information to their subconscious.

Exercise 1 - Receiving Information

Wherever you are at the moment, look up from the book and take in your environment. Let your eyes relax and just glance around. When you are done, look back at the book or computer screen and don't look away again. Choose a primary colour, either red, blue or yellow, close your eyes and try to remember what you can in your environment that was the colour you choose.

Open your eyes and have a look around. More than likely there will be many obvious objects that you missed. When I perform this exercise with students it's not uncommon that they miss objects right in front of them or large objects in the room. What does this prove about distortion?

It was much easier to see the coloured objects when we were actively looking for them with your eyes open obviously. However,

> during that moment for sure you didn't notice any of the other two colours. Your conceptual mind focused your attention on one thing only, blocking out other information. It essentially distorted the real information to serve a purpose.

THE R.A.S SYSTEM

Your brain has a part called the *Reticular Activating System*, or R.A.S. for short. Its job is to act as a filter and only let through valid information. The information that gets through is based on a few different things. It can be information that we are actively looking for or focusing on, as in the exercise above. It can also be information that conforms with our beliefs and it can be information that we have pre-programmed in our subconscious as we will explore in the next chapter; *Visualisation*.

Why is it there? *The Encyclopaedia Britannica* reports studies that estimate the body is receiving 11 million bits per second of information through the senses. However, in tests it seems the brain is only capable of processing 50 bits per second. For example; when concentrating on reading, that equated to about five words per second that are read, digested and imagined. That is an enormous amount of compression that is taking place, or in other words; filtering of information to what is relevant at any moment in time. If our brain was to take in and process all of that information at once it would probably explode. Therefore the R.A.S. has to decide what it lets through to be processed and guess what; the R.A.S. is programmable just like a computer.

Of course, this can be a good thing as we discussed in the chapter on focus. However, if you are distorting information to fulfil a negative belief you have of yourself, you have more than likely entered the vortex of self-fulfilling prophesy. This is when you begin convincing the inner-self of something by actively looking for the information to back it up, ignoring the rest.

THE EGO

Before we look at how a real self-image is formed, we have to be aware of three major common ways you can distort it. Your essential self-image is the one at the centre of your being, and essentially the one that your actions will derive from. It can be influenced positively or negatively by a thing called the *ego*.

The ego is a delicate mechanism. It sits in the outer part of the self and is partly responsible for what the inner-self hears. The ego is right on the border between the conceptual self and emotional self, just before the R.A.S. In fact, you could argue that it is part of it. Before the conceptual self is allowed to analyse anything, it has to pass through this filter. An embarrassing event such as a bad shot under pressure, in front of others or a collapse when you should have won, hurts the ego. It can shield you from the hurt by deflecting the embarrassment away or it can turn against you by blaming the inner-self in order to protect itself. If you want to look truly at yourself you should detach yourself from the ego.

If you let the ego deflect incoming criticism away from you it can hinder learning and progress. Information that may be useful for growth may not be allow to manifest in the conceptual mind. This is someone who responds to an insult with an insult. If someone criticises you and your response is; "idiots, what do they know" and an attack on them follows, your ego is deflecting.

Likewise, turning against your inner-self and joining in is detrimental to you as well. This is how *what you think others think of you* can produce a negative self-image. Others say "I am bad at this" so I simply agree. The ego never likes being wrong, so it will confirm the other's opinion in order to satisfy itself. "They're right" it will say, "you really do stink at that."

With the ego taken out of the situation, we can merely acknowledge the event and look at it logically. This is our best chance to do something about it. Fox et al. 2014, describes the following three traits of a self-image which I believe the ego is responsible for.

Customizing - If allowed to expand it will become selective about what aspects it chooses to do in the real world and what challenges it will undertake, selecting only those it knows it will achieve. This can be a player who only plays with others who are worse than them or never leaves their home course. It's a method of staying in the comfort zone because the ego will not let you risk failing. This type of player will find it extremely difficult to improve because they are never prepared to take the next step into the unknown.

Presentation - This is where the ego pretends to be something it isn't. It's concerned with convincing others that you are whatever, whether it may be true or not. It gravitates towards looking a certain way in order to present to the world an image that the ego wants. This also works the same internally, presenting it to your subconscious. You may have heard the phrase; "all the gear and no idea." That player fits perfectly into this category, so does the one that unnecessarily talks themselves up. Telling everyone how great they are and even lying or exaggerating about results, all to portray an image that in reality is not congruent with who they really are.

Bias - This is a filtering process which starts by selecting only the information that conforms with its beliefs and similarly avoids those that does not. It's a form of distortion and works both ways, negatively and positively depending on the opinion the ego has formed. More commonly it can be seen as a player who dislikes a certain hole. The drive for example, doesn't fit their eye and they believe each time they play that they will hit out of bounds. Their ego is customizing the information in order to protect itself from disappointment. Hofseth et al. 2015, refers to this as *self-handicapping*. It's when someone sabotages their preparation in order to justify the outcome. For example; a golfer decides to break from what they normally do or have planned to do, such as a warm up or pre-shot routine to use that as an excuse in case they fail. A bias ego loves excuses, it's never their fault.

YOUR TRUE SELF-IMAGE

The image you have of yourself on the golf course is defined by three major influences:
- What you think of yourself
- What you think others think of you
- What you would like to be or expect

What you think of yourself - This is the long hard look in the mirror that many of us shy away from. Firstly, it's made up of how you see yourself physically. Are you fit and healthy? Do you like your appearance? More important than good looks and chiselled abs, are your golfing muscles optimal? Are you flexible, stable and strong for golf? The conclusions you came to during our self-analysis in chapter 1 should have given you a starting point from which to expand on.

Secondly, what about your golf intelligence? How much do you know about correct golf technique and more importantly, what works for you? Do you consider yourself a wise strategist on the golf course? Are you are someone that looks back on their round of golf with regret, wondering why they hit that driver on number fifteen, or why they went for the green on number three before the round had hardly started. If so, you are at risk of having poor self-golf-intelligence.

Thirdly, it's also effected by what you think of your technical skills. "I can't play that shot," indicates a gap in your ability to perform a given task. If you go ahead and attempt it anyway that just shows poor golf-intelligence, but recognising a lack of skill can be self-derogatory if not accompanied with a plan to do something about it.

Finally, your moral self-image has a big part to play in golf. The obvious is anyone prone to cheating. However, on a deeper level it is the feeling of deserving what you receive in the form of results, prizes and praise. If you believe that luck (or dishonesty) was the only reason you were successful then you can attach no responsibility to it and subsequently can't claim any of the praise. If you cannot justify the morals of attaining what you have then you are less likely to respect it. Just look at how lottery winners squander their money compared to business owners who have worked hard for their millions.

Exercise 2, Part 1 - Paint a picture

The first step of improving your self-image is to start to identify with it in an honest and objective fashion. The first task is to write down a list of everything you think about yourself. Use the four categories above as a template. Think of yourself physically, for example; you may be flexible but have weak legs. Write down *all* of the positives and *all* of the negatives, you are going to need them for later on. Do the same for your intelligence, skills and morals and if you can link things to your life outside of golf, even better. Keep this list extremely private, it's what you think of yourself, nobody needs to know these thoughts.

What others think of you - Because golf is played in the public arena, you are always on display. Whether it is with fellow playing partners, a few people watching around the first tee or huge crowds of spectators, your inner-self knows it is being judged. All sports psychologists that refer to self-esteem or self-worth agree that the sportsperson should detach themselves from their performance. I think more importantly you should detach yourself from results, which are mostly out of your control. Performance is determined by your effort. Knowing that we are not perfect, it's only an accumulation of our physical and psychological skills, a perfect performance can only be judged by whether or not you gave it one hundred percent. If that is the case your performance was as good as it could possibly be that day. The result depends on many other factors such as luck and your opponents.

However, you can easily be judged by others according to your result or ranking. You may have performed to the best of your ability and still be branded a loser. In theory that shouldn't be negative to your self-image, but pressure from outside can affect what the subconscious receives. This effect depends very much on how your conceptual self filters this information. It can choose to let criticism and insults from outside sources through, or it can block and filter them into something useful. If we let the ego do this it will distort the information, it must be done with an open curious mind.

> **Exercise 2, Part 2 - Continue the painting**
>
> Part two of this exercise is to write down a list of what you think people think of you. Start with golf and all of the people in your circle. For a club golfer this might be the group or society they normally play with, the members of your golf club or friends and family. For a professional golfer this could include fellow competitors, staff working with the associations, the media and the public. Again, write down all of the positives and negatives. Examples could be: *The public thinks I'm brilliant, the press thinks I'm arrogant, my friends think I'm insecure, my competitors think I'm a perfectionist, etc.*
>
> Expand this to your whole life and note any links between the two. Then highlight or underline those which you really agree with. It might be all of them or very few, but do it without the ego. If this exercise is kept private as mentioned before, there should be no reason to involve the ego. Nobody knows but you.

What you would like to be / ideal self - We instinctively create an image of who we want to be, but more often than not in a way that doesn't help us. It's bad for your self-image if you are constantly comparing yourself to someone else, unless there is a plan in place that motivates you to progress. However, comparing yourself to your future ideal self is very powerful if done correctly.

It needs to be SMART; Specific, Measured, Achievable, Realistic and Timed. If it lacks any one of these your ideal self will probably be out of reach and only cause frustration. Being out of reach is the same as having expectations which are too high. It can lead to anger initially if they are not achieved and with time it damages the self-esteem as you cannot live up to who you want to be. If done properly it can be a powerful motivator and help you in the decisions you make or the way you react to situations.

Exercise 2, Part 3 - The Greenfee

Imagine two golf courses you have never played but would give your right arm to have the chance. Probably they will be famous golf courses you see on the TV such as Augusta, St. Andrews or Pebble Beach. It can be any two, just select them and write down the names. Also, select three playing partners who you would love to play with. They can be anybody, friends, family or famous golfers past and present, or a mix of all. Write down their names too, this is your ideal game of golf. The weather forecast looks good, nice temperature, it doesn't get any more perfect than this.

When you arrive at the clubhouse to check in on the morning of the first game, the reception doesn't ask you money (or your right arm). The payment for this game of golf is you have to trade one third of all the thoughts you had about yourself in the first two parts of the exercise. Take a pencil and draw a line through each of the thoughts, positive or negative that you want to discard. You will only play golf today with the remaining thoughts of your self-image, the others don't exist anymore.

You move on to the second course and the next day the same thing happens when checking in again. The reception asks for half of the remaining thoughts on your list. Draw a line through them and you'll only be left with approximately thirty percent of what you started with. Imagine playing this second day with only that self-image. You would have probably deleted the negative ones by now and possess only your best qualities.

This exercise requires you to look at the positives in your self-image and forces you to decide really what is important to you. It's a big step in deciding how you could be a better version of yourself. With such a perfect two days of golf you would obviously want to be the best self you can be, you wouldn't want to ruin it by taking a bad version of you along. If you can picture playing golf and living your life with these fundamental qualities you have taken a step towards deciding your ideal self.

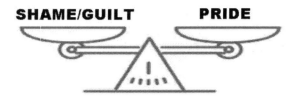

MORE EMOTIONS: TOO MUCH SHAME/GUILT

Guilt, shame and pride are some emotions which have a big influence on the self-image. Although both guilt and shame sit at one end of the scale, they are actually slightly different. Guilt can be described as a feeling of responsibility or remorse towards a certain event, act or behaviour. This is the more common of the two in golf. It involves a very dangerous word; *should*. I think it was an old Steven Spielberg movie Amistad, about African slaves where I heard a quote from one of the tribal leaders. He said; *"in our language we do not have the word; should, we either do or do not, it either is or it isn't."* That wasn't the exact sentence but it was something similar. It struck me how true that phrase was and how many times we used the word in our western lives. *"I should have hit another club, I should have warmed up properly,"* and the negative version; *"I shouldn't have gone for the green, I shouldn't have gotten angry.*

Looking back with regret and wishing you could change an event not only produces guilt, it's just plain insanity. Science pretty well shows we live in a space/time continuum, so until they do invent a time machine, I'm afraid what's done is done. Or better still, what's in the past stays in the past. If we understand fully that there is no changing an event that has taken place, we can leave it there, learn from it and move on.

Shame on the other hand is a more serious issue. Shame is the painful feeling when reflecting on who you are. Shame makes a person want to escape and hide. This shows a damaged self-image, regretting who you are or not living up to who you expect to be. Embarrassment contributes to this feeling and can have more effect over time. For example; missing an easy two-foot putt, especially an important one or hitting the dreaded shank. These are golf's way of testing our self-image. We can react in a way which identifies it as an *anomaly*, shrug the shoulders and realise it's just a part of golf. Or we can let it intimidate us and chip away at our self-image. If the latter is what you do, you are shaming yourself based on a result.

Shame and guilt are on an emotional scale, so we must recognise they do play a part and need balance. These emotions are what helps us recognise right and wrong. They are what is referred to as pro-social emotions. Although they are dependent on the environment, which means that right and wrong depends on the core beliefs of the person. For example; the strongest and most violent of a street gang could hold themselves in high self-esteem if that is what their environment requires. However, golf has built in rules and etiquette to the game. These rules make it fair for everyone who plays. For most people breaking these rules will inflict guilt or shame on the perpetrator. The emotions of guilt and shame help to keep us inside these boundaries.

The good thing about guilt is it can produce a desire to repair that which is broken. It is needed anytime you find yourself using the word *should*. If you should have hit a different club, the initial guilt to recognise the mistake and followed by a logical, not emotional, analysis will lead to fixing the problem so it is less likely to happen next time. I would suggest to start by replacing *should* with the word; *could*. By using the word *could*, you are not invoking guilt, it suggests there were other options but you just choose the wrong one. Next time I am in a similar position I *could* choose another option which may have a better outcome.

TOO MUCH PRIDE

Down the other end of the scale there is pride. Pride has had a bad reputation over the years, being known as the original and most serious of the seven deadly sins. Not only Roman Catholics have this thought, it can be found in most of the world's religions. In Hindu it is one of the *Arishadvargas* relating to arrogance called *Mada* and in Buddhism one of the five *kleshas* or poisons. They all come to the same conclusion, too much can cloud the mind and result in unwholesome actions.

Too much pride is quoted by Dante to be the *"love of self-perverted to hatred and contempt of one's neighbour."* In Latin it was called *Vainglory* which later evolved to *Vanity*, meaning unjustified boasting. Although all of the above sounds bad from a religious standpoint, golf is a competitive game not a religion. Religion has the roots of recognising one is humble in the face of God, therefore pride is obviously challenging that very aspect. A balance would be humility, without slipping down to low self-regard or unworthiness.

Feeling like you are better or superior in a competitive environment can't be a bad thing. We need to feel pride in who we are, but more so pride in what we do and that we deserve to reap the rewards. I don't think this is a bad thing and certainly isn't corrupt selfishness. Pride in who you are is a powerful emotion, especially if it is strongly linked to your core beliefs. Like all of the emotions it has to be kept in balance.

EXERCISES TO IMPROVE SELF-IMAGE

Returning back to the subject of this chapter, let's look at effective ways you can change your own self-image for the better. Remember, as we discussed earlier, your self-image takes a long time to develop and is the accumulation of many different factors. However, by doing the following exercises regularly, we can feed the inner-self the healthy food instead of poisons. Be patient and commit to each of these at least once per week, it will be effort worth spending for your general well-being.

Exercise 3 - Keep a Journal

Keeping a journal for a period of time or indefinitely is a great way to notice all of the positives during your day. It requires a little bit of homework to get started. After each round of golf take a few minutes to yourself at home and reflect on what you experienced during the day. You don't have to answer all the following questions every time you play, but read through them and note anything that stands out.

What one shot or type of shot did I play really well today?
Where did I get lucky today?
What did I accomplish today, referring to any process goals that I have?
Did something fun or humorous happen today?
Did I see something someone else did that I liked?
What am I thankful for today?

By thinking of and writing down a brief answer to any of these questions you are focusing on the positives that made you happy. Noticing these aspects of your day all add up over time and influence the self-image you have. We know that you can't change your self-image with a command, it takes a long time to establish whatever self-image you currently have. However, constantly reminding yourself of what you like about yourself is a start to changing it.

Exercise 4 - Perfect Golf

Perfect golf is best done as a form of physical practice on the golf course. It's a technique I originally used with beginners when venturing out to the course the first few times, but soon realised it was just as beneficial psychologically for any standard of golfer.

To do it alone requires having a good understanding of strategy and what you are trying to achieve with each shot, especially what the target is. For this example, we will use the twenty percent rule, although you can adjust this depending on your standard and expectations. This means that you have a margin of ten percent each side of the target on every shot. A two-hundred-yard drive will have twenty yards either side, a one-hundred-yard approach has ten yards, a thirty-foot putt has three feet and so on. Putts inside nine feet have to go in the hole.

Now we have the parameters set for a successful shot, when you have the chance on your home course, replay any shot until you have the ball within your margin. Please be aware of any fellow golfers you have behind you and any rules your golf course may have regarding practice. However, usually it will not take any more than three shots to hit your shot to an acceptable place. You'll actually be surprised how many times you hit your acceptable target with the first attempt.

This exercise has many benefits. It helps to stop perfectionism as you have a realistic target objective. Not all drives will finish in the middle of the fairway, not all putts from twenty feet will go in, but if they finish close enough you can congratulate yourself on a good attempt. It also helps in forming strategy on the course (as we'll see in the strategy chapter) but most importantly it fills you with the confidence that you can achieve each given task. Even if it takes you a few attempts, you learn or make some adjustments if not successful the first time and can quickly identify the types of shot which cause you the most problems. This can later form part of your practice and improvement plan.

Psychologically by finishing every shot with a success this exercise can't fail to give you a sense of hope to what your potential can be on the golf course. Unfortunately, we are not perfect, we will make mistakes, that is part of golf and how we manage mistakes determines our overall performance. But realising that you can achieve any shot makes you feel good and does wonders for your self-image.

Exercise 5 - Back pocket punishment

This exercise delves into the dark and mysterious area of self-punishment. It doesn't involve whipping ourselves and drawing blood to release evil spirits or anything to that extreme. However, it does involve recognising negative thoughts and making yourself uncomfortable for thinking them. In the psychological novel *The Monk Who Sold His Ferrari* by Robin Sharma, he explains how the monks in his character's village would walk nine miles through the mountains to stand under a freezing waterfall if they entertained any negative or destructive thoughts. A harsh punishment one could say for merely thinking the wrong thing, but they argued that thinking the wrong thoughts was far more punishing in the long run than the hassle of feeling cold and wet. The monks soon learned to abandon quickly any form of negativity towards others or themselves. Later the character explains how he had a bracelet with beads on which he would take off and remove a bead for each bad thought. At the end of the day he could tell whether his mind was productive or not by how many beads were left on his bracelet. An empty bracelet meant he'd had a poor day with a weak mind, a full bracelet showed a strong and productive mind.

The golf version of this doesn't require cold waterfalls though. Golfers usually carry tee pegs in their front pockets for hitting the drive on each hole. For this exercise you are required to place one of those tees in your back pocket every time you let a negative thought develop. By develop, I mean recognise it and allow it to linger. We will learn a technique in the chapter *Confidence* which can solve this problem. However, if you have had a negative thought and found yourself still thinking about it after the first few seconds, put a tee peg in the back pocket. Negative thoughts can be about a particular hole, a shot, playing partners or anything related to your game.

Once the tee pegs are placed in the back pocket they must stay there until you are home and change out of your clothes into something else. This has two effects. Firstly, it is really annoying to sit down with tee pegs in this pocket. Each time you sit in a buggy, on a bench or in the clubhouse afterwards you will be reminded that you must not entertain these thoughts. It gives another meaning to; *a pain in the backside*, because the negativity is what you are portraying to others and your inner-self. Secondly, at the end of the day you will have a physical representation of the amount of times you let your mind wander into undesired territory. It can be a great reminder of how little control you have over your thoughts and if your mind is helping you or hindering you.

Chapter 5: Visualisation

"Visualisation is daydreaming with a purpose" - Bo Bennett

INTRODUCTION

We are all culprits of daydreaming, letting our mind wander through imaginary scenarios, having make believe conversations with people and doing activities. The question is though; is it productive? Visualisation is nothing more than daydreaming but with a specific outcome or a pre-planned script. It's your own little movie inside your head, it's private and you are the director. In fact, you are the director, the actor, the sound guy, costume and make up, everything.

You may know an actor by the name of Jim Carrey. Known for his outlandish comedy, he has also starred in some of the biggest box office hits over the last couple of decades. He explains on many occasions in interviews how he went through troubled and difficult times as a child growing up. As a young man he wanted to act and make people laugh, this was his passion, but maybe one could argue, his escape from the life he was presented with as a child. When his shift at work finished, he used to drive through Los Angeles up to a place called Mulholland Drive where all the rich and famous had their big mansions. He'd park up his car on the side of the road and get out just to stand there and imagine being one of them. He would imagine being successful as an actor, having fans, attending Hollywood parties and everything else that would come with show business.

One evening in 1985 whilst running through one of his dreams he imagined being so much in demand that a production company would pay him ten million dollars for a role in a movie. He found a pen and paper in his car and wrote a check to himself for that exact amount for acting services rendered and dated it ten years in the future. In 1995 after a few successful movies he was offered the role in the hit comedy *Dumb and Dumber* for, you guessed it; ten million dollars. He stresses though, it's ok visualising your dreams, but then you need to work hard to make them materialise. "You can't just visualise and then go eat a sandwich," he says.

I relate to this story just because of the sheer coincidence of what happened to Jim. However, many others report the same mindset and vivid visualisations of their future. Michael Jackson and Madonna used to wish upon a star every night before going to bed, Michael Jordan used to visualise taking the winning shot in every game. Can it all be coincidence? Or is there some truth behind these unseen powers of the mind?

THE UNIVERSE WILL CONSPIRE

Actually yes, there is lots scientific evidence. We mentioned in the last chapter a part of the brain called the Reticular Activating System or R.A.S. Its job is to filter all of the information coming in through the senses to an amount the brain can manage to process at any given time. Therefore, it excludes almost all of the information and only processes a tiny amount which is turned into thoughts and memories. The good news is, the R.A.S. is programmable, we can direct it towards that which we want processed. The phrase; "water, what water?" is our mind directing this part of your brain to only see the fairway. One of the most famous self-help books in history, *Think and Grow Rich* by Napoleon Hill is mostly mistaken to be a book about money and wealth. Those that understand its hidden message knows the book is not about how to get rich, it's about how to use your mind to achieve what you desire.

Through visualisation we can program the R.A.S. to be on the lookout for those things that are important to us. More good news is the R.A.S.'s database is huge. We don't have to have one goal or desire; we can have many. We can run many scripts of different scenarios, different goals and desires and with repetition they all get stored. When the R.A.S. is programmed in such a way it will notice that information which conforms with our program and process it instead of something else. I think this is what the philosophers mean when they say the universe will conspire to make your dream a reality. It leaves a conflict between your subconscious and reality, so your brain automatically tries to resolve this conflict. It tries to fill the void by finding the information that it believes it wants.

When you think about it, every action, every word we speak, everything starts as a thought. We can't do anything without our brain sending a signal somewhere to make it happen. Some are reflexive, our heart beating, digestive system etc. or a response to a stimulus. It's still a signal coming from the brain but it's just generated automatically without us having to conjure it up. Some are conceptual, meaning we have to initiate the sequence with a conscious thought. When you get out of your chair, the sequence either starts with a little voice in your mind saying; *initiate standing up movement*, or you create a picture of where you would like to move to. The brain then finds the relevant blueprint from its database and the signals are sent to start the action. The exact same process happens when you play a golf shot. You create an instruction and your brain has to access a blueprint in your memory as to how your muscles should move in order to hit the ball. So, if everything we do is started by a thought, wouldn't it make sense to make sure that what is entering our brain is information to help us create the correct thought.

DIRECTOR VS ACTOR

When visualising there are two common methods used. Being the director of the scene is where you see yourself performing the outcome that you desire. During this scenario you are sitting in the director's chair and watching the scene you have created be brought to life. As with all visualisation techniques the more vivid the picture, the stronger its effect will be. The director will have planned the background, the sounds and character details such as the clothes you are wearing. You will see yourself portraying the emotions that you want, the look on your face, your body language and mannerisms. You control the camera too. You can see yourself from any angle and at any speed, slowing the picture down can help you see the finer details.

If playing the part of the actor, you place yourself in your body. You see the scene through your eyes. This can be especially powerful because you can add in more senses. Feel the wind on your face, smell the freshly cut grass and more importantly feel the movements and emotions that you want. A good actor not only recites lines from a script, they play the part physically and emotionally. Anthony Hopkins is known for rehearsing his lines hundreds of times so he can forget about what he has to say and concentrate on the subtle emotions and actions which makes his characters so convincing. Remember earlier how I explained that memories are much stronger when associated with strong emotions. If we can place ourselves in an imaginary situation and really feel the emotions which help us succeed, our memory of that occasion is more likely to be catalogued above others.

Either technique works well and many successful athletes use a combination of both. They see the scene from the director's view first in order to design and rehearse the outcome they would like. They then play the scene again but this time placing themselves in the action and becoming the actor.

WET VS DRY

The term wet and dry when talking about sports comes from Olympic swimming terminology. Dry refers to the practicing of movements and positions outside of the pool, whereas wet refers to being in the pool. Since hearing these terms I have always referred to any practice away from the golf course or driving range as *dry* practice, therefore any striking of the ball becomes *wet* practice. With visualisation any mental rehearsals that we perform whilst at home or in the hotel room are dry, any visualisation techniques we use whilst playing or practicing are wet.

VISUALISATION IS VISUAL?

The word visualisation is a little bit misleading; it entails that it has to be visual. In reality you can visualise with any of the senses. Musicians tend to be very auditory in their visualisation. They can hear notes and beats without any music; they can create music in their heads. Ludwig Van Beethoven is famous for the fact he wrote some of his masterpieces towards the end of his career whilst almost, if not completely, deaf. He described that he understood the patterns or mathematics of music and with that he could visualise hearing the sounds in his mind. A chef is most likely gustatory-visual, being able to imagine how something would taste.

In golf, during wet visualisation, the most common way is visual. Science suggests that we have become much more dominant with the visual sense since the turn of the information age over the last forty years or so. The ancient humans had more balance between their senses and that didn't change much during the industrial revolutions. However, the information revolution, which has been increasing ever since the first computers, has dominated our world with screens and visual stimuli. Therefore, most people find it easier to picture something rather than use the other senses. However, pretending how the shot will feel before you play it is just as valid as picturing it. This is making use of the tactile-sensory system, which is touch and more precisely the proprioception-system, which is the awareness of your body in space and time.

In fact, if we think in depth about everything required to make a golf swing, it might look like this: the visual sense is used to judge and calculate the shot's distance, shape, etc. The tactile sense is giving you information on current conditions, for example; the strength of the wind blowing on your face. As you take your stance over the ball, the vestibular sense kicks in; it helps keep our balance and posture. At the same time, the proprioception system is keeping us aware of where our body parts are, where we are holding the club, how far from the ball, etc. Starting the swing heightens the kinaesthetic sense, which reports information on how our joints and muscles are moving. The tactile sense will then give us feedback on how the strike felt, if it was central and there is no vibration, if it was too hard or too soft. All of these senses literally layer upon each other as we get closer and closer to hitting the ball. So, when it comes to visualising a certain shot, we have an abundance of senses to choose from. Most people will only use the visual sense when asked to visualise but it can be a more complete experience if we can include other senses as well. Imagine how it feels to make a certain movement in your swing, the sensation through your hands when hitting a crisp strike.

DRY TECHNICAL PRACTICE

Dry practice is the daydreaming element of visualisation where we run through scenes in our mind. Much like the techniques of hypnosis, it requires us to be relaxed, focused and undisturbed.

A form of dry visualisation is imagining changes in our technique whilst away from the course. The exercise below, Exercise 1, describes how to practice away from the driving range and achieve just as good, if not better, results than physically being there with a club in your hands. It is a very powerful method which encompasses *Timothy Gallwey's* theory of change only happening when it has our *full awareness*. Without the distractions of actually hitting the ball or worrying about others watching you, we can give the changes we want to make our full attention without fear of failure and in the comfort of our own home.

Exercise 1 - Can you feel it?

No, it's not singing The Jacksons hit from 1980, but I liked the name so I stole it. The exercise involves using physical keys of what you would like to change and then your imagination to reinforce the change. Generally, after a good coaching session with your professional, you will have come to a conclusion involving one or two key points regarding your technique. These key points are usually to prevent a bad shot from happening or to produce a certain style of shot; i.e. ball flight.

The most effective way of changing a motor action, the blueprint of the movement that is stored in our subconscious, is to create a new version. The easiest way to break a habit is to make a new one. If we can combine the physical sensation from doing the action with repetitions in our mind, our mind will still be sending those signals and creating the memories we want. The beauty of this is you don't even need to move; the signals still get created and sent whether you end up doing the action or not. This exercise can be practiced anywhere, at home, in the office or anytime you have a few minutes spare.

The first step is to physically perform the action. Pretend you have a club in your hands if the key is something to do with your arms or wrists. Otherwise you can just cross your hands across your chest if you want to focus on your legs or body position. Do the action slowly, keep your eyes open and check the position. It might be that you're trying to keep your posture steady and the professional has told you to make pretend swings with your head against the wall. It might be that you're trying to keep your left arm extended as much as possible. Whatever the key is, stop, check it, do it slowly and meticulously. Repeat this five times.

The second step is to perform the action again, however this time with your eyes closed, relying only on the physical sensations of the body. With your eyes closed it increases the awareness of your body in space and time. If you have to, stop and open your eyes briefly to check the position is correct. Repeat this five times also.

The third step is to stand in your set up position again, but this time you are not going to move. Close your eyes and just imagine the movements from before. Visualise what it looks like, feel the movement, but only in your mind. You may find that your body will move very slightly or twitch. Your thoughts are still sending the signals to your muscles even though you instructed yourself to stay still. Repeat this as many times as you like until you lose focus.

With this new blueprint installed in your memory, you can access it anytime you want. Even sitting in a chair or lying in bed at night. By visualising the changes, you want to make and being linked to physical keys, the memory is strengthened every time you do it. You can also integrate this exercise into your practice on the driving range by performing it between shots. It's harder to do because of the many distractions, you have to keep your mind on the task at hand, which is changing motor actions, not the quality of the shot. Run through the routine and then hit five balls, focusing only on the physical key, don't worry about where the ball goes. Refrain from all judgement about the shot, the only focus should be on the body sensations.

Exercise 2 - Be your own shrink

To work effectively, it is recommended to follow a consistent framework when performing this type of visualisation. Try to find a dedicated time each day in the evening or morning when you can be alone for a short while. It doesn't have to be every day for it to work but obviously the more repetitions you make the better the results. To work best we need to plan at least fifteen minutes of quiet time to ourselves, sit in a comfortable chair or lay down on the bed. Free from any distractions we can use a relaxing and focusing exercise like the Relaxation Exercise 5 in chapter 2. Once we are calm and focused our body and mind is now in optimal condition to start a visualisation scene.

Below I will give an example of a basic transcript for a visualisation session. If you have a good memory or once you have learned the exercise you can talk yourself through the process. You cannot look at notes once we begin, so to start with I recommend you record the transcript with your own voice onto your phone or other device and listen to it.

There are five phases you should pass through on your journey:

1) Relaxation

Sit in a comfortable position on the sofa or lay on the bed, remove all distractions and dim the lights if possible.

I'm placing my focus on my breath. Breathing in through the nose, starting now to the count of four...1...2...3...4...and exhale through the mouth slowly, again to the count of four. Repeat this one more time...2...3...4...and exhale...3...4

As I inhale, I can feel my stomach rise...3...4...and as I exhale my chest sinks and relaxes...3...4

On the next exhale my body sinks further into the chair/bed...as it relaxes...and again 2...3...4...and relax 2...3...4...inhale...and relax...all the tension is drifting out of my body

2) Internal Focus

In a moment I will start to count backwards from 5...With each exhale my eyes will begin to close...and fall further into total relaxation

Inhale and...5...my legs and back feel soft, sinking, relaxing

Inhale and...4...eyes start to feel heavy and sleepy

Inhale and...3...all those little muscles in my neck and shoulders feel soft, sinking, relaxing

Inhale and...2...my face, jaw and eyes continue feeling heavy, sleepy

Inhale and...1...eyes are now closed, relaxed, body sinking, heavy, relaxed

Breathing slow and deep, I feel peaceful, relaxed, breathing, sinking, relaxed

3) Director visualisation

Picture the place on the golf course where everything takes place...I can see the grass and landscape...I can see the flora...the sky...I can see myself...moving slowly and deliberately

I can see myself smiling, laughing...but my posture is tall...I look confident (or whatever trait you would like to see) *...I look comfortable...but relaxed...I like this image of myself...it suits me*

It is time to play...I can see the look on my face change to one of business...determination...focus

I can see myself going through my pre-shot routine...taking my practice swing...it looks effortless...smooth and controlled

I can see my eyes narrow...totally focused on the target...it looks calm and self-assured...total focus...unwavering focus

As I step into position over the ball...it's smooth and precise...looking like it's been done thousands of times before...one last look at the target

The swing starts...slow and smooth...(insert here the swing keys you are working on if you have any) *...beautiful tempo...rhythm...the strike is crisp...the sound is crisp...the finish is perfectly balanced*

I can see the ball heading off towards its objective...it was always going there...from the moment it was decided beforehand...I see a small grin on my face...subtle but visible

Congratulations are exchanged...I nod my head in acknowledgement...once again I have seized the moment to do something special...it was my moment

4) Actor visualisation

Breathe deep once again...exhale and relax

Now I'm looking through my own eyes...I can see the grass and landscape...I can see the flora...the sky...I feel myself...moving slowly and deliberately...I can feel the breeze on my face, the grass crunching under my shoes

I feel happy, smiling, laughing...there's no better place to be...my posture feels tall...confident (or whatever trait you would like to see) *...I feel comfortable...relaxed...I feel good about myself...I like this me*

It's my time to play...I can feel the muscles in my face relax...no more smiling...it's time for business...I'm analysing the variables of the shot, distance, wind, target...and choosing my club...time to focus

I perform my pre-shot routine...taking my time...this is my moment...when I'm clear of my objective I take my practice swing...it feels effortless...smooth and controlled

I can feel my eyes narrow...totally focusing on the target for a few seconds...I feel calm and self-assured...I'm ready to execute

As I step into position over the ball...it's smooth and precise...left foot stepping out first...then the right foot...I've done it thousands of times before...my head turns for one last look at the target

I feel the club move away...slow and smooth...(insert here the swing keys you are working on if you have any) *...beautiful tempo...rhythm...the strike feels crisp through my hands...the sound is crisp...my finish is perfectly balanced...total control*

As my head comes up, I can see the ball heading off towards its objective...it was always going there...from the moment it was decided beforehand...I feel a small grin on my face...a grin of satisfaction

I hear the congratulations...I nod my head in acknowledgement...once again I have seized the moment to do something special...it was my moment

5) Pretending it's already done

I feel the confidence in my ability reinforced...I feel more confident than ever

I take a brief moment to feel the satisfaction of another great shot...it'll happen again soon...of that I am sure

On the count of three my eyes will open and I will come out of this scene

1...I can feel my fingers and my feet start to move
2...I feel the confidence in my ability
3...My eyes are now open and with it I feel self-assured and confident

The above transcript can be adjusted for any scenario, any shot, shots or feelings that we want to experience. I would like you to take the time to think of parts of your game or psychology you wish to improve and adjust it accordingly. It may be to feel more bravery and less fear, more calmness or less anger after a bad shot. If you choose a scene in which you are responding positively to a bad shot, don't include the bad shot in your visualisation. We want to refrain from any negative aspects in our visualisation, so start the scene once the undesired result has happened. Then deal with it in the positive way you would like, for example; by feeling angry and then quickly accepting it and moving on to a great next shot. Follow that with a feeling of satisfaction at how you dealt with the adverse situation and you have created a great memory to access when the situation arises in the real world.

WET VISUALISATION

Wet visualisation happens when playing the game. It forms part of our pre-shot routine during every shot we play. Unlike the actor who mentally rehearses their part and then repeats it when the lights, camera, action is called. Unfortunately, golf has no script, no matter how much we plan. Every shot is different, the distance, the club, the shape. Every day the conditions change, the wind, the speed of the greens, firmness of the ground. Whereas dry visualisation prepares us for likely scenarios, wet visualisation is the dynamic, on the fly version.

It has to be fast and efficient; we don't have time to enter deep relaxation. However, it has to be crystal clear and as free as possible from any distraction. It sounds like a tall order, but with practice it becomes easier and eventually routine. If we use our time on the practice range correctly, we can integrate visualisation into our game and seamlessly take it to the golf course. Jack Nicklaus said that he never hit a golf ball on the course or in practice without vividly having a picture of it in his mind beforehand. He was arguably the greatest competitor the game has ever seen, although not technically the best. He beat everyone and won a record eighteen major championships with mostly his mind. If he wouldn't attempt to play a shot without visualising it first, then perhaps we should do the same.

A VISUALISATION BLUEPRINT

Jason Day says how he has to close his eyes in order to picture himself making the swing he wants but describes it more as a feeling. He can feel the swing, the path of the club and the sensation of the hands. This type of player is more kinaesthetic in their approach. Jack Nicklaus however, explains how he played his own private movie. He could picture not only his swing, but a vivid image of the flight of the ball, where it would land and how it would react when landing. Essentially the shot was already played before he ever stepped up to the ball.

If we are going to integrate visualisation into our pre-shot routine it should be with the method you feel most comfortable. You can find this out by using it first on the driving range or by taking note of which feels easier to do in the director/actor experience in exercise 2 of this chapter. If you can mix both visual and kinaesthetic that would be ideal, but not essential. However you go about designing your visualisation technique, try to include as many of the following points as possible.

A clear picture of where the ball will land. Some people can imagine how the ball will react once it lands but this depends on the level of the golfer. High level golfers can control the ball flight and spin; therefore, they will have a good idea what will happen upon landing. They will expect a bounce left or right, where the ball will run on the green and how much backspin will take effect. This level of detail is not necessary for most golfers, but it is important to know where the ball will land.

An image of which direction the ball will fly. Every level of golfer should be able to envision how a perfect shot will fly to the target. This is very personal because everyone has a different style of shot. For a fader of the ball the flight will start initially to the left, then curve to the right towards the target. The opposite will happen for someone with a natural draw. How much the ball will curve is dependent on the severity of the players natural shot or the shot they are trying to play.

The height and trajectory. The club you are using will determine the initial trajectory and height of the shot. This goes together with the direction to build an overall flight path which the ball will take.

Any visual or kinaesthetic keys you have for your swing. You can picture this visually or imagine it as a feeling. It can be key points for a great swing or key points to achieve the shot shape that you want.

The above four parts make up a great visualisation routine. It doesn't matter in what order they appear. You can start with the swing and see the shot in chronological order or you can work your way backwards from the target. We'll discuss in the *Preparation & Energy* chapter how this can fit into your pre-shot routine in a quick and smooth way. However, before using visualisation in competition it is recommended to practice it like you would any other shot on the driving range.

Whilst practicing, use a portion of your time to practice randomness. This is where you select a club and type of shot at random similar to what you'll experience on the course. During this time, it is important you are free from technical thoughts, we want to encourage a playing situation, not a technical one. Once selected, go through your entire pre-shot routine. Use this time to practice your ability to visualise the shot. Pick a target, construct the visualisation, have a practice swing and play the shot. It should take twenty seconds maximum. Afterwards you can analyse if the shot resulted in what you had envisioned. If it didn't, repeat it until it does. Whilst practicing this way you can adjust the visualisation without the fear of failure until you find something that works.

In conclusion, visualisation is not a one size fits all subject. There are different types of visualisation, that which you can do away from the course and whilst in the arena. Although they have the same objectives and their technique is very similar, their use is completely different. However, you decide to integrate visualisation into your game, it must be a wholehearted effort. It takes repetition, practice and more repetition to get good at it, then followed with a plan of how to achieve it - you can't just go eat a sandwich.

Chapter 6: Confidence

"A man cannot be comfortable without his own approval" -
Mark Twain

"What we could accomplish if we knew we could not fail" -
Eleanor Roosevelt

Mark Twain and Eleanor Roosevelt have summed up confidence very well with the above two quotes, although there was a third which I refrained from putting into the title because it's written in a negative form. It is a quote from Suzy Kassem, a modern day American-Egyptian philosopher who states; *"Doubt kills more dreams than failure ever will."* It is essentially the negative half of Eleanor's *"What we could accomplish if we knew we could not fail."* If we subtract one from the other, we would be left with a clear definition of what confidence actually is; an absence of doubt in anything that we do.

INTRODUCTION

Let's say I asked you to jump on the spot with the only objective being that you landed approximately in the same place. Would there be any doubt in your mind that you could achieve the task? Of course not. You would make the jump, which had no requirements such as how high or what the other parts of your body should do, and then probably look at me with a *what now?* expression on your face. What would happen if I asked you to jump but this time spin around three hundred and sixty degrees and land back in the same place? Would you doubt your ability to do that? Maybe, but I know some snowboarders who wouldn't think twice about performing that action. How about jumping as high as you can, making a full upside-down flip and landing back on your feet? I think most people would doubt their ability to do that. Although for sure there are circus performers who would confidently accomplish the task with no doubt at all.

The point I am trying to make is not that believing you can do an upside-down flip is going to make it possible, if you attempted that now you'll probably break your neck so please don't. Our confidence is very dynamic, situation dependent and naturally unstable. We need to convince ourselves beyond doubt that we can do something and that takes various ingredients to do so. If you play golf with limited confidence it all starts with identifying what is causing you to have doubt. It may be in general or it may be in a specific situation such as a bunker shot, short putts or first tee drive. Sports psychologist Bob Rotella says; *"Given two players of equal skills, the more confident one will win nearly all the time."* It's almost overwhelming to think of it that way. No matter how good your technique is or how much you have practiced, if you're not confident with what you can do, someone else will probably win.

CONFIDENCE IS NOT AN EMOTION

Confidence doesn't appear on any of the emotion scales presented in this book. It clearly has an opposite, doubt, so you could argue that it should have a scale of its own. However, neither confidence or doubt is a feeling, it is a belief. If someone says that they *feel* confident you can interpret it as a misunderstanding or arrogance. Arrogance is false confidence. It is overestimating your abilities even to the point of being ignorant about the consequences. I would be totally arrogant if I attempted to jump, back-flip and land on my feet. It would probably end in tears. However, if confronted with two hundred yards of carry over a water hazard, I would whip out my four iron and not have any doubt at all I could make it to the other side. That's not to say I wouldn't miss-hit one and end up wet, we are not perfect, but I know I have the ability to match the given task.

Confidence can't be felt, it is knowing that what you are doing is right. It is purely blank or white. If there is any grey then doubt is present. This is the dilemma when dealing with confidence in sports and especially in golf. Standing over a three-foot putt we know realistically that every now and then one of them will miss, but should that logic affect your confidence? It should not. In fact, the chances are so high that you will make the putt it would be silly to even entertain the thought. If it does miss it should be regarded as the *anomaly*, the imperfection of being human and nothing else. What is far more important is all the ones you successfully holed. This is the premise of successful experiences discussed below.

During coaching, if somebody says to me; *"I feel confident,"* about a certain shot or part of their game, I will challenge that thought by asking where does that feeling come from. If they back up their claim with a mixture of the ingredients that make up confidence then I will believe them. By demonstrating how convinced they are about it I will understand that it wasn't just arrogance talking. If they say *"I've lost my confidence,"* I'll ask where they left it, like a set of car keys. Where was the last place you had it? Maybe an ingredient or two has been lost, not the whole confidence. This way you can think of confidence as a tangible asset, something that you can own if you pay the price for it, in other words, do the work.

If confidence and doubt are not emotions then we don't have to manage them like we do with fear, anger, etc. With true emotions the objective is to keep a healthy balance between each side of the scale. However, with confidence we want it tipped one hundred percent so that no doubt at all is present. So, if confidence and doubt are not naturally occurring emotions and are a belief system instead, below we will find out how to systematically build them like you would with any other belief you have.

INGREDIENT 1: UNDERSTANDING THE TASK

In order to have no doubt at all we have to fully understand everything about the task and how to meet it. We naturally fear the unknown and that leaves ample room for doubt to creep in. If we understand what the task requires and have technical and theoretical knowledge of what is needed then we are less likely to doubt. The perfect example could be a player who comes for a lesson on bunker play. On countless occasions I have asked the player to perform a few shots to warm up and from the onset it is clear they do not know the correct technique for playing out of the sand. The clubface is closed or the ball is positioned back in their stance like a chip and there is no wonder why they can't get the ball out. They say they are not confident in the bunker, but really it is a lack of knowledge that is the problem. Once they understand how the clubhead reacts in the sand and have a clear picture of how everything works, even before practicing it physically, confidence has been installed in their ability to achieve the task. Whatever it may be, driving, chipping, playing under pressure, research the topic fully. If you don't know how or can't find the information, that is what golf professionals are for. The first step in any improvement is understanding why and what you are trying to achieve.

INGREDIENT 2: SUCCESSFUL EXPERIENCES

Good memories from successful experiences are the vital ingredient like yeast is to make bread. However, these memories don't have to be real, they can be simulated. This is where good use of your time practicing can be a huge benefit. Also, it is why visualisation techniques such as those in the previous chapter are important.

There is no doubt that positive real experiences do wonders for your self-confidence. Whether it is winning an event or just a certain tee shot on a hole, positive experiences feed more positivity about the future in every psychological way. Once you have achieved something just one time, it is all that is needed to convince yourself that you can do it again. It is why we see so often first-time winners, whether it's a major championship or a regular tour event, repeat their success again very soon afterwards. Phil Mickelson springs to mind, after so many near misses at major championships and having the unwanted monkey on his back of being the best player not to win a major, he broke through in 2004 at the Masters of Augusta. Once he had the achievement accomplished, he quickly went on to win many more soon afterwards. He had confidence in himself that he *could* finish off a major championship, even after all the times he had thrown one away previously.

Using that example, we could argue that if you have ever made a three-foot putt, of which I am sure everyone has, why would you ever doubt your ability when faced with the challenge again. This is where successful training experiences play a part. Quite often we need extra convincing of our efficiency to complete the task, in other words, tip the odds in our favour.

Exercise 1 - Tipping the odds - A formula for confidence

An important part of your practice is proving to yourself you can do whatever it is that you are trying to do. Let's take the example of the player in the bunker from before. Once they understand what it is they are trying to achieve, it is time to experience it in the real world. To do this we need to break everything down into simple but progressive tasks.

Step 1 - The process would start with a no pressure situation. Unlimited balls, unlimited swings, let's just see if you can hit one shot out of the bunker using the correct technique of sliding the clubhead through the sand, under the ball with enough speed and loft so the ball explodes out with the sand and clears the lip of the bunker. Once achieved you can tick the box.
I can now do this properly [ ]

Step 2 - Now you need to prove to yourself this wasn't just blind luck. To do this we again use unlimited attempts but this time you have to hit two correct bunker shots in a row. Once this is achieved you can confirm to yourself that you now have the skill that you desired and tick the next box. It wasn't a fluke,
I'm on to something here, it wasn't just luck [ ]

Step 3 - Add some limitation. For example; use only ten balls and count how many successes there are. Do this a few times and record your best score. The next time you come to practice repeat this step again and record the score. This provides undisputable evidence of improvement if the scores are getting better over time. It appeals to your conceptual part of the brain which likes the data and translates that as confidence to your inner subconscious mind. If there is no improvement it is only a sign that something is not quite right yet and you may need more help or more time to get used to the changes. The goal here is only to try and beat your best score. Once you have done that once, tick the next box.
I'm definitely getting better [ ]

Step 4 - Add pressure. The idea of practice is to simulate and prepare for the real thing. Once you are comfortable with the new experience and confidence is rising you should test how well it holds up under pressure. In this step you can challenge yourself to hit a certain number

of shots without failure. Start with an easy number such as five and build it up each time you practice. When adding a rule to start again from zero you will be increasing the pressure on yourself each shot you arrive closer to the objective. Nobody wants to fail on the last one and have to start all over again, although it will happen sometimes. If you finish a practice session with this achieved it can not only install confidence in your ability to do the task, but also to do it when it matters. I have had keen students spend hours on a putting challenge only to fail and go back the next day with even more determination than ever and succeed. When overcoming such levels of frustration and pressure to achieve the task it has to make you feel confident in your ability to do it when you have to. The trick is to make the challenge attainable and not too difficult that it hurts confidence, but not too easy that you don't get a rush of satisfaction once it's completed. That's why you should start small and increase the difficulty as your skill heightens. Each time you complete a challenge tick the box.
***I can do this when it matters* [ ]**

Adapt the exercise to whatever part of your game you would like more confidence in. It's not limited to physical skills such as bunkers or putting, you can use the same techniques for any encounter. I believe desensitization plays a big part in developing confidence and too much fear can hold you back. Stepping outside your comfort zone and having a moderate success can make you realise *it's not that bad*. In fact, any sort of success outside your comfort zone has to install confidence, it is what leads you to accept the next challenge thereafter. It may be playing your first tournament or playing with better players. For a high-level golfer, it could be beating the local competition before venturing out to national championships and then international tournaments. Organise the achievements into bite-sized attainable tasks and you will feel much more confident when presented with the next.

Also, in this section I would like to add the influence of others success. Being involved in other's success or simply watching it can install confidence that something can be done. We have all heard of the four-minute mile. Previous beliefs were that man could not run an imperial mile (or 1,609m) in less than four minutes. However, when Roger Bannister accomplished that task in 1954 it was soon followed by others who now had the belief that it was possible. We see this in professional golf. Mark O'Meara played on tour from 1984, spending two hundred weeks inside the top ten of the world. He won multiple events all over the world but until 1998 he never won a major championship. A few years before that he befriended a young upcoming golfer who had attained some success in the amateur ranks. They struck a relationship that has been described as O'Meara being a surrogate father, helping the young guy feel his way into professional golf. The young guy had big dreams as all young aspiring golfers do, O'Meara's job was pass on his experience as a master would do to their apprentice. The youngster turned professional in 1996 and won on tour in his fifth tournament, but that wasn't enough, he wanted a major. This was being explained to a forty-year-old, who had played on the tour for twenty years and still hadn't won a major. He must have been thinking; how do I teach this kid patience, there are hundreds of players out here who have never won a major. Considering all the players and only four opportunities per year, the chances are pretty slim.

The first major of the year came around and the surrogate son said he believed he could win it, even if it was his first major championship as a professional. He not only won it, he demolished most of the records set by all the games greatest golfers during the century before. Of course, if you hadn't guessed it yet, the surrogate son was Tiger Woods. Although the significance of the story is that Mark O'Meara won that Masters championship the following year, as well as the British open championship a few months later. O'Meara attributes a lot of his success that following year to the inspiration Tiger had on him, the Master. I believe there are two reasons for this which are both founded in confidence. Firstly, by witnessing the belief the young apprentice had in his ability to win made O'Meara realise that was the only thing holding him back. By learning to believe he could win the ultimate prize in golf it gave him the confidence to do so. Secondly, by being Tiger's practice and playing partner he undoubtedly beat him on many occasions away from the media coverage. I can picture them having putting competitions and bets on their home course where O'Meara was the winner. While all of the media coverage and the world of golf was placing Tiger on a pedestal, making him the feared monster he became when playing, his master was quietly kicking his backside on a regular basis. Just imagine what this would do for your confidence. He knew he could beat what many were already proclaiming as the best golfer the world had ever seen. Funny enough, later that year in 1998, O'Meara met Tiger head-to-head in the final of the World Matchplay in Wentworth, England. The dual of the master verses the prodigy finished in the master's favour.

A similar example can be made of two good golfing friends who burst on to the scene in recent times. Justin Thomas and Jordan Spieth grew up competing against each other as junior golfers, both being exceptional at a young age. Jordan though, was the first to break through, winning on the PGA tour as a teenager and the first to do so since 1931. Two years later he won the Masters at Augusta and followed that with the US Open. He could have easily won the remaining two majors as well. All this while his close friend was just progressing from the lesser Web.com tour on to his first year in the main league. In the height of Spieth-mania, Thomas recorded his first victory at the end of that year and went on to dominate the tour in 2016-17 where he also won a major. It could be down to pure competitiveness between the two friends, but I believe that Spieth's success showed Thomas would could be achieved by someone no different to himself. It was a case of; *if he can do it, I can do it too.*

INGREDIENT 3: POSITIVE VISUALISATION

When discussing the topic of confidence, it is clear that success early on in a golfer's career helps to breed more confidence. Many international superstars we see on the television set started dominating amongst their peers throughout their junior days, into their amateur stretch and naturally carried on with the confidence gained into professional golf. However, there are many stories of winners who didn't taste success until later in life. Players like Padraig Harrington and Ian Poulter didn't have spectacular junior and amateur careers and yet still exuberated confidence when playing professional golf. In their minds they didn't have the memories of beating all the competition numerous times, at least not the real memories.

As we explored in the previous chapter *Visualisation*, they found confidence through imagined memories, which can be just as effective. Poulter had already dreamed big since the day he was sitting in the local pro-shop selling chocolate and decided he knew what he wanted from life. He had undoubtedly envisioned himself being a Ryder Cup hero and winning clutch holes with the whole world watching. It's the team camaraderie of the Ryder Cup which is what inspired him to play as a profession, not the individualistic gain which golf is commonly known for. Harrington, a qualified accountant, dreamed big because he didn't want to be sitting in an office all day, despite choosing that career path in his studies. They are good examples of the Jim Carrey effect explained in that chapter.

Positive visualisation can involve both the dry and wet versions of the topic, such as creating scripts and scenes of success away from the course, or using visualisation as part of your pre-shot routine. The key here is to make sure they are *positive*.

Exercise 2 - Your Palace of Success

This is a dry visualisation technique, meaning it's done away from the golf course in the comfort of your own home. Similar to the exercise script in the *Visualisation* chapter, it is recommended that you lay down or sit in a comfortable chair, relax and focus internally for a short period first for it to have the best effect. Also, record your own voice so you can play it back or memorize the exercise so you can talk yourself through it.

Once you are in the right state with your mind and body, I want you to imagine a familiar place. It can be anywhere but a place where you would regularly be and see family or friends. It could be your local golf club, a bar, or even your own home for example. The familiar surrounding helps the immersion because it's something you can picture easily and feel comfortable in.

However, this time as you walk into the familiar setting there will be some changes. There will be signs of your success everywhere. These signs can vary depending on what your goals are and of course depending on your level of golf. For a low handicap or club golfer they could see their name up on the club championship board or see the trophies of club competitions sitting on their mantel piece at home. They could see photographs in the local paper of them winning a local event. Think of as many different ways as possible and flood your chosen setting with these images. Add to this an auditory stimulus. As you walk into the setting people you know start congratulating you. *"Great golf the other day mate,"* one says, *"Well done, you deserved that,"* another one expresses.

For a professional it could be seeing a report on the national news about your success in a big event. It could be a party in your honour with friends and family. You could walk into your local club and see one of those giant cardboard cut outs of yourself promoting a ball or equipment. Posters of yourself, framed photographs that you have signed or heads turning as you walk into the room.

During one of the congratulations somebody asks you if you felt nervous or how you managed to win. You respond to this by talking about the amazing birdie you made at the end in order to clinch

> the title. Describe to them what you did and how you felt. *"I was playing really well but it was getting very tight,"* you explain, *"but I was confident I could finish it off. I had a great feeling down the stretch, like something good was going to happen."* Make up anything you want, it's your dream, your success. Make it seem as real as possible.

The beauty of this exercise is it mixes something present and real such as the location and the people with something desired. It makes the visualisation ever more real and gives you a sense that it's not out of reach. Practiced regularly it can give you a sense of Deja vu when you do eventually get into a position to win. You may not have all the success stories of Tiger Woods, but we can create as many as we like. The subconscious doesn't know the difference, they are all just memories as far as it's concerned.

Wet visualisation, that which takes place during the game and most commonly used in a pre-shot routine, is an obvious place to be positive. However, we are only human and negative thoughts will enter into the equation at some point. It is a common mistake to believe that what makes great golfers great is their overwhelming confidence and positive thinking. They are good at it, but like the majority of us, they are still prone to negative thoughts every now and again. The difference is not that they don't have negative thoughts, it is how they deal with them. Once a negative thought sneaks in, it is quickly identified as one and steps are taken to dismiss it. After all it is only a thought, it should hold no significance to future events unless we allow it to. If you are susceptible to self-handicapping yourself in order to excuse yourself or give the ego satisfaction for being right then you'll let the negative thought manifest. If it is truly recognised as a stupid thought and nothing more, then you can get back to the business of planning your shot correctly.

> **Exercise 3 - Counteracting Negativity**
>
> A practical way of dealing with negative thoughts on the golf course is to use the counteract method. It involves replacing any negative image with a ridiculously positive one, dismissing them both and getting back to the job at hand.
>
> I first came up with this technique whilst playing some competitive golf on a local tour. There was a period where I admittedly

had doubts about my chipping. It was no problem out of semi-rough where there was margin to brush under the ball. However, when playing from a tight lie around the apron of the green the problems would start. I could trace it back to a tournament we had played a few weeks prior. The local tour was played during the winter months in the south of Spain where the climate was mostly sunny and warm compared to the rest of Europe. Although, the golf courses were usually heavily watered and soft and any rain would only add to the softness. Tight shaved grass, soft ground, delicate chips on fast greens and after a couple of fat ones it's only natural that confidence was starting to dissolve. We played a particular course which had recently dressed the areas around the greens. Dressed in maintenance terms is when they lay down a lot of sand mixed with seed in order to dry out the soil and grow more grass. It is a common practice in tropical areas especially in the spring when the growing season starts. For a nervous chipping action this was a recipe for disaster.

A negative thought would run through my mind each and every time I was faced with a chip. I knew that a stubbed chip was up there with the shank in terms of shots a professional shouldn't hit, but I had lost confidence altogether by this point. Something had to be done. I knew my chipping technique was good, my set up, my angle attacking the ball was fine, I could do it whilst relaxed practicing by myself. It was the thoughts, or to be more exact the negative memories that were causing negative projections about the future.

So, when faced with a chip and catching a negative thought entering my mind, usually involving a duff, I started to counteract the thought with a ridiculously positive one. I said to myself; *"I could hit it heavy, but then again I could land it right there, it'll bounce once, take the break left and go in the hole."* I would then finish the thought by saying; *"but they are only thoughts, I don't really know what is going to happen, so let's get back to playing the shot."*

Little did I know at the time, the last thought holds much more strength in the subconscious mind. I hit the chip and it went in.

That's no exaggeration, however I must stress, it's not a magic formula that'll make you hole every chip you encounter. There is no golden ticket when it comes to golf, but being in a good frame of mind doesn't hurt you. Later, when I analysed and tried to make sense of what had happened, I discovered two significant keys to why that technique was successful. Firstly, it forces you to recognise they are just thoughts. Everything starts as a thought. A negative one is harmless by itself (in moderation) but if we allow it to manifest it increases fear or doubt which in turn leads to a physiological change. Tightening of the muscles or miss-timing is ultimately what results in bad shots. Therefore, by identifying it as a thought, you catch it before the chain reaction starts. Secondly, as stated before, the last thought you have holds more weight. By replacing the negative with a positive the latter is the one that lingers while you go about your business of a pre-shot routine and playing the shot. How many times have you thought about making a long putt, completely forgotten about it, only to hole it later when it's your turn to play?

The key to this exercise is to use it immediately as soon as a negative thought appears. The sooner you catch the thought, counteract it with the positive and then forget about it, the better it will work. It applies to any shot. If it's a drive, imagine the drive going straight down the middle and twenty yards further than you normally hit it. Any shot approaching the green would go in the hole, that's the best possible end anyone could wish for. Dismiss both thoughts as only that which they are and get back to playing the game and not trying to predict the future. I'm not saying don't have a plan. The pre-shot planning is vitally important as we'll see in the next chapter, but we are not fortune tellers. If we could accurately predict the future there would be much better uses for it than worrying about a golf shot.

INGREDIENT 4: POSITIVE SELF-TALK

To explain the importance of positive self-talk I will first quote a paragraph from Bob Rotella's great book, *The Golfer's Mind*.

Suppose, for a moment, that I was applying to work as your caddie. "What would you do for me besides carry the bag?" you might ask.

Suppose I answered: "First of all, whenever you hit a bad shot, I'm going to say, 'Terrible! That was terrible! How could you hit such a pathetic shot? You choking dog!' If you hit another bad shot, I'm going to get on you worse. 'You can't even play this game' I'll yell. 'Why don't you give up?' Then, at night, I'll come to your room and remind you of all the mistakes you made that day. And the last voice you hear before falling asleep will be mine, saying, 'You stink!'.

You would, of course, tell me to go away and never come near you again.

That is a brilliant representation of what goes on in the majority of golfer's heads. It poses the question: would you talk to anyone else like that? If you did, you probably wouldn't have many friends. Nobody likes being around the company of people that criticises them and brings them down. In fact, just about every self-help book, no matter the topic, warns you about these types of people. Yet, we become one of these people as soon as we start talking to ourselves.

Bob Rotella goes on to explain that you need to start talking to yourself like you would to a child. You wouldn't dream of yelling at a child who's only trying to do their best. Instead you would try to encourage them. You would say; *"Come on, you can do this, you're a great player."*

By changing what we say to ourselves, it can have a huge impact on the self-confidence we create for ourselves. Remember, the inner-self, subconscious mind can't distinguish real or not real, positive or negative. It only believes what we tell it. And make no mistake, if we are constantly telling it that it stinks at golf, it will believe those words. Instead, it would be wiser to tell it that you can achieve the task at hand. That you have done it before, that you deserve it more than anyone else, that it is possible.

I understand that it can hurt when disappointment arrives. *You can do this, you can do this* - only to be followed by a bad shot or poor performance, can be painful. But great players use that disappointment to fuel improvement. They use failure to figure out why, then do something about it. It's much easier to say *I'm pathetic* and accept that is what life gave you, but that is the mentality of a loser. Yes, it's less work and it also satisfies the ego who predicted that you would fail. It is much more difficult and much harder work to identify the reasons for your failure and correct them. Despite all the pain it causes, that is the winner's approach.

In conclusion, try not to worry about the pain of disappointment. Encourage yourself in every way that you can, but realise, like a learning child, that you are not perfect. Accept that things will not always turn out right, but don't insult your inner-self when that happens. Be kind to it, tell yourself that *next time it will be better, I believe in you.*

INGREDIENT 5: POSITIVE SUPPORT

The last major ingredient to building confidence comes from the support of people around you. Most professional athletes have a team even if their sport is individual such as golf. However, recreational golfers also have, a more unofficial team around them, even if they don't know it. A professional's support team may comprise of a technical coach, nutritionist, physical instructor, psychologist, manager, etc. These people not only help the player in the traditional ways of transferring their expertise and knowledge in their given field, but they also form a bubble around the player which reinforces the belief that they are getting better in every way and are ready to be successful.

Whereas a good quality coach should be installing confidence in their student through the progress they are making together, whether in practice, in the gym or in other ways, support also comes from your friends, family and peers. Golf is a wonderful sport where it is not uncommon to see players helping and encouraging each other even though they are competitors.

You should treasure the people around you that offer their genuine support. Likewise, you should offer encouragement and support to others. Having a family or partner who wishes you luck and still believes in you, no matter the result is of vital importance to building confidence. Many times, the support we need is all around us, we just don't recognise it or in some cases challenge it. *"Good luck darling"* one says. *"Yeah, I'll need it,"* comes the response. That is classic self-deprecating humour which does no good at all for confidence. When someone offers their best wishes, the confident person would think; *I don't need luck, I am good enough to win without it,* even though they would probably not say it out loud. Is this arrogance? Not if you firmly believe it and it's backed up by other ingredients.

The confident person loves the praise others give them; they never dispute it. There is no need to show it. The inner-self is the one that needs it, not the emotional or conceptual self. When your peers, team or family congratulate you on a great shot or game, take it to heart. Say thank you out loud, but tell your inner-self you deserved it. Don't, for the love of all that is good, dispute it or assign it to luck. Accept praise because you understood the challenge, you had practiced it in advance, you had visualised it anyway and you had told yourself through self-talk that you could do it.

Chapter 7: Strategy

"The essence of strategy is that you must set limits on what you're trying to accomplish" - Michael Porter

INTRODUCTION

The more your physical golfing skills improve the more important it is to understand strategy. After all the balls hit on the range, the hours spent getting the body and mind ready, strategy is the final piece which completes our preparation. Without an understanding of how golf strategy works we are leaving a lot to chance when it comes time to conquer the golf course.

CONE THEORY

Cone theory is what I call it, I definitely didn't invent it and don't know who did. It goes by many different names but many of the greatest golfers have described it in one way or another as how they approach the challenge of getting around a golf course.

Simply put, if you asked someone to hit ten balls with each club and then viewed the results from above you would find that the further the ball finished away from the person the wider the dispersion would be. You could draw an almost perfect cone each time extending away from the golfer. The basic physics involved means hitting the ball with more speed and a straighter faced club results in the ball travelling further offline even if the discrepancy at impact remains the same. There's nothing we can do about this, despite advances in technology over the last few decades.

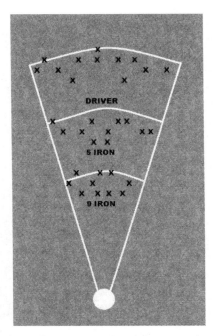

If we took this a step further and followed the curvature of the ball during its flight, we would also find that the majority of the time the curve would be going the same way. Some people would have a right to left shape (a draw) and others would have a left to right shape (a fade). There are many different reasons for this and a general misconception is that one is better than the other. In truth, either one is good, if you can reproduce it consistently.

Ben Hogan said; *"You only hit a straight shot by accident. The ball is going to move right or left every time you hit it, so you better make it go one way or the other."* Making it go one way or the other depends on many factors. A person's anatomy as well as technique can affect whether they are a natural drawer or fader. Having an overly dominant side can affect how you attack the ball, just as having an overly dominant upper or lower body. This is getting into the subject of biomechanics and outside the scope of this book, however it is important to establish your preferred shape and hit it as consistently as possible.

Exercise 1 - Which side of the bed do you sleep on?

Okay, it's nothing to do with your sleeping habits, although it's normal for couples to always sleep on the same side of the bed, even if they are away in a hotel. This is where you feel comfortable and it allows you to sleep better. In golf you need to find the side that makes you comfortable too. To do this, head to your local practice facility with an alignment stick, piece of bamboo or old broken shaft. Make sure it is something you don't mind breaking just in case you do hit it with the ball. Line it up perfectly between your ball and

A PRACTICAL GUIDE TO GOLF PSYCHOLOGY

the target you have selected in the distance and take a few steps forward and stick it into the ground so it stands up straight. It should now split your practice area down the middle.

Start with a middle iron club and choose a side to start the ball. The objective here is to curve the ball back towards the centre line or the target in the distance. Play ten balls and then switch sides. Very soon into this exercise you'll have a feeling for which side feels more natural to you.

Once you have decided the side which feels best, starting right or starting left, try to make it so the ball never crosses the centre. For example; if the ball is starting left, it should always finish on that side. If it curves a little to the right towards the target, that's great, it's called a fade. You're in the same category as Jack Nicklaus, Colin Montgomery, Dustin Johnson to name a few. However, if it crosses the line, it's now moving away from your target. That is a slice and puts you with the rest of the weekend hackers. If the side you selected is right, it would be nice to see the ball curving left back towards the centre. This is a draw, you're now with the likes of Ernie Els, Lee Westwood and Ben Hogan. If it crossed the line it becomes a hook. Strategically we never want the ball moving away from the target. This is the problem with trying to hit the ball dead straight. It's always going to be moving away from your target unless you can play golf like the Iron Byron robot they use to test clubs.

CONE THEORY MATHEMATICS

Cone theory can be made into very simple mathematics for use on the golf course or when planning a round. Scott Faucett, a very good golfer himself and a very in-depth analyst of golf statistics with his decade system, describes golf as having a shotgun, not a rifle. It would be very nice if we could think of our game as having a sniper's rifle and see the target in our crosshairs each time, but unfortunately that is not the case. In reality our shots take off in the general direction but scatter all over the place, like a shotgun.

I've found by working with a percentage of the distance we can easily calculate the likely area of dispersion. If you fired a shotgun into a wall one metre in front of you, you would see many marks from the shrapnel close together. However, if you stood at five metres, the marks would be scattered considerably wider.

Scott records that professional golfers who drive the ball three hundred yards have a dispersion area of sixty-five yards at best. That is roughly twenty percent of the distance, or ten percent each side of their target. So, let's say you are an average golfer who hits their drive two hundred yards, your dispersion area will be forty yards wide if you have good control with this club. If you want to get very precise with these measurements, I suggest using a shot radar which will track the ball flight for you and give you all the necessary statistics. However, a good rule of thumb would be twenty-percent of the distance, give or take a couple of really bad swings. Improvements with swing technique and practice we can bring the dispersion area down, but it will always exist.

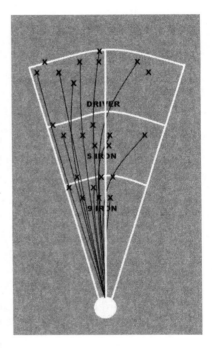

If we can consistently control the starting direction and curvature, you will start to see that the majority of shots group together and form a bias on one side of the cone.

The big difference with the top level professional is that they have a very strong bias in one half of their dispersion, as to say; one half of their cone contains the majority of their shots. This is the importance of practicing the above Exercise 1, you develop a control and understanding of your ball flight and the probabilities of where it will finish. There will always be a few shots that escape and cross the line. These are slippage from the norm, but if ninety percent or more of our shots finish in the bias area then we should have a good idea of what to plan and expect from any given shot. That is why I used the quote from Michael Porter at the beginning of the chapter. On its surface it may seem a little negative saying *you must set limits on what you're trying to accomplish*. However, for golf this is the essence of a good strategy, knowing your limits and more importantly, the *probabilities*. It defines the area where your ball is likely to go, only then can we build a strategy around it.

This is what is referred to as a *stock shot*. A term that gets thrown out there a lot by golf commentators but is never actually explained with much detail. In fact, you have to be very careful with what is said by golf commentators in general. Don't get me wrong, I appreciate they have a very difficult job trying to keep us entertained and informed for hours upon end. However, sometimes their technical analysis is a little off or they use jargon which confuses the issue they are trying to address. Scott pointed this out in a short video I saw, where the commentators were talking about Dustin Johnson's improvements over the years. One said, that he had become a better player since he had eliminated the shot left. Scott went on to dig up the statistics on Dustin's driving accuracy over the years which showed he missed in the left rough more than most other players on the tour and had done for most of his career. In no way had *eliminating the shot left* affected his rise to being the world number one player.

I'm going to give the commentator the benefit of the doubt though. I think when he said the *shot left*, he was referring to a hook. Dustin's strong grip and closed clubface throughout his swing probably resulted in undesirable hooked shots when he didn't want them, especially under tournament pressure. Dustin has consistently hit a fade for many years now and has described in interviews how he likes to start the ball up the left side of the fairway and let it slide back, similar to how Jack Nicklaus played. This means that when he hits it too pure and the ball holds its line straight it is likely to finish left of his target, but is by no means a hook. Dustin actually does completely the opposite of what the commentator said, he eliminates the right side because his ball always starts left and moves back to the target, it seldom moves right of it. If it does, he still has half of the fairway that side at his disposal. His bias in his cone is the left side, missing the target left is just part of his game. What he should have said was; *Dustin has eliminated the miss right*. That would have been much more accurate.

Here we find the single biggest factor which holds most people back. It's called perfectionism. Someone striving for all zeros on their trackman results is ignoring the whole essence of the game. It's not about hitting perfectly straight golf shots, it's about consistently controlling the flight of the ball so you can at the very least, roughly predict where a shot is likely to finish. That is how you get around a golf course. Golfers are only a good as their misses. Let's see how we can take cone theory out on to the golf course.

CONE THEORY: DRIVING

Once we can control which side the ball is likely to finish, we can use this information on the golf course when planning a strategy. We need to take into consideration the bias of our cone when standing on the tee. Not just direction though, distance too. Most par fours and fives are designed in a way to catch the longer drive, therefore sometimes hitting your maximum distance may not be the best option. The smart golfer who understands this will identify it immediately and base their strategy around avoiding that danger. After all, golf is nothing more than avoiding the obstacles, then getting it in the hole as fast as possible. If our very first shot of the hole finds penalty areas we are always playing catch up and that's not much fun.

Often, I challenge players that I am teaching who tell me they are driving the ball poorly. "How many penalty shots did you have as a result of your tee shots?" I ask. If there were penalty shots, they were more likely a result of poor strategy and choice of club than it was a poor swing. There is no denying, we all love to crush a drive right out of the sweet spot but the reality is, while it does give you a little boost of confidence, it doesn't make any difference to the score that goes down on your card. If you are playing only for that rush, that quick fix of satisfaction, then I'm sorry but you haven't yet grasped the concept of the game. I know that seems a bit harsh, but I presume if you've made it this far into a golf psychology book, you are probably not one of those people.

A GOLFING PHILOSOPHY

My overall golf philosophy is summed up as: *After the drive, you only need to hit one good shot to make a par.*

What? *That's crazy* you might think, but let's analyse that statement for a minute. On a standard par four where you can reach the green with your second shot, if you hit a good one it should be on the green and within a close enough distance to the hole to get down in two more shots comfortably. You have a par.

If the second shot was poor (but strategically correct, as we'll see in the next section) it will miss the green. However, if you hit a good chip it should finish close enough to the hole to be almost guaranteed. Thus, resulting in a par.

If the chip was not good enough, you have one last option and that is to hit a good putt, which means it goes in. That's only one out of three shots that need success in order to make a par. If you hit two out of three it'll probably result in a birdie. I admit, this is a very simplified philosophy of what actually happens on the golf course, but there is an important point to note. Notice it reads: *After the drive*. This concludes that the drive doesn't matter whether you hit it good or not, it just needs to be in play. It only needs to be in a position where you can start the process.

I learnt this the hard way and it wasn't from a coach or a sports psychologist, it was from my wife. I was playing a tournament in Cyprus and had played myself into contention after the first two days.

On the final day my swing felt tense, it wasn't the free-flowing swing I'd had the rest of the week. I had become obsessed with not striking the ball well, which was most notable with the longer clubs of course. She was caddying for me the final day but had not seen me play during the week, so I was trying to explain to her that I was missing the middle of the club constantly and that was why I was getting agitated. Despite being a magically beautiful sunny day on an amazingly scenic golf course, she could tell I wasn't enjoying it much because I felt like I was playing bad. That was the problem, I *felt* like I was playing bad, but was I really? Striking and playing are sometimes two completely different things. The score represented a bad round too, which in turn backed up that belief.

At the end of the round, which funnily enough finished on a high with an eagle, I commented to her that I hit the ball terrible, especially the drive and there was no surprise I shot a high score. To which she responded; "I didn't see you in trouble all day long." Hang on a minute, I thought, she was right. I went back and analysed the round and found I hadn't hit my tee shots into any trouble all day. Not one penalty shot from the tee. The bad score had come from the rest of the process, not getting it in the hole fast enough. The fact that I wasn't crushing my drives like I was on the previous days hadn't made any difference, just a psychological one. The *feeling* that I wasn't playing well, where playing well really had nothing to do with it.

From that day on I was a little more sceptical about the importance of the drive. Don't get me wrong, it has to be good enough to get you in play. In elite professional golf the courses are so long and especially in major championships, the rough is so high, driving long and straight becomes an advantage. Although, it never decides the winner. In amateur golf, driving long and straight is not all that important, the fairways are more generous and the holes are much shorter. Unimaginable amounts of money are spent every year marketing and promoting drivers. The promise of longer, straighter drives will revolutionise your game, knock five shots off your handicap, blah, blah, blah. They know your ego desires that new driver, but remember, they want your cash. They will convince you that driving is the most important part of the game. The price tag sure represents it. People will spend large sums of money on the new driver and having it custom fit, all whilst having old putters and wedges still in their bag. For sure, splash out if you can afford it. A little improvement in technology here or there can definitely make the game more enjoyable, but don't expect it to be a game changer, no matter what the poster says. I compare the drive or tee shot now to a goal kick in football (soccer). It gets the play going, what happens after determines whether the team scores a goal.

So, with all that said, we need to have a strategy that gives you the highest probability of getting the play going. It starts with identifying the danger side. Using our cone theory and your bias we can design a strategy that gives you the greatest chance of starting the process described in my philosophy.

DIRECTION

It is very rare that you find a golf hole that has severe, penalty shot danger on both sides of the fairway. Unless the hole is very short and has little other protection, or is badly designed and squeezed into the planning of the golf course. Most however, have one side which is regarded as the bailout side. It may be rough, there might be a few trees to contend with, but it's definitely better than going to your bag for another ball.

By understanding our tendencies, we can plan to get the ball in play and make the challenge as easy as possible. Here is an excerpt from Jack Nicklaus' book *Total Golf Techniques*:

"The toughest shot in golf is one that's perfectly straight. It's tough to execute physically because so many things must be exactly right at impact. It's tough strategically because it reduces the target area - if you aim at the centre of the fairway, then hit a slice or hook, you have only half the fairway to play with, whereas if you aim, say, down the left side and play for a deliberate fade, almost the full width of the fairway is at your disposal if you overdo it."

What does he mean by the *full width of the fairway?* Isn't the fairway the same size for everyone? Visually it is, mathematically it's not. Let's imagine the fairway is thirty yards wide, which is roughly the width of most fairways. The first player is trying to hit a shot dead straight down the middle. However, they do not know if the ball is going to curve right or left. Either way, there is only fifteen yards of room each side before the ball misses the fairway. Imagine there is also water or out-of-bounds on one of those sides, they are truly playing roulette now.

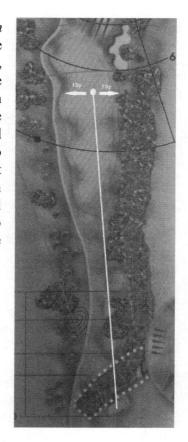

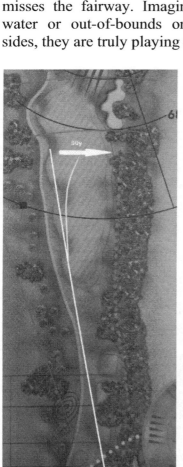

The next player, who purposely shapes the flight of their ball aims down the edge of the fairway. If they naturally curve the ball towards the centre of the fairway it is very unlikely it will curve the other way. If the ball continues straight with no sidespin it'll finish on that side. If the ball curves like it usually does it will be heading back towards the centre. If it curves too much they still have fifteen yards of room before it reaches the other side. Bearing in mind that the bias shows this happens a minimal amount of the time, we would expect most of the shots to finish on one side of the fairway. As long as their initial flight starts along the edge of the fairway as planned, they have essentially doubled the amount of room the ball is allowed to curve during its flight before it reaches potential problems. That is what Jack means when he says *full width of the fairway at your disposal.*

DISTANCE As mentioned before, it is not always the wisest decision to go for maximum length. Holes are usually designed in a way to protect them from overpowering. Many fairways start to narrow at a certain distance. From professional competition tees this is usually around the three-hundred mark. Playing from amateur or ladies tees the distance will be shorter. Knowing how far your driver, three-wood and long iron or hybrid travels with a good shot is important to know if it will reach these areas and run out of room. The player should also assess the risk of doing so. We don't want to play defensive and leave unnecessarily long second shots all of the time, but if there is potential danger waiting up there, is it worth the chance of finding it? Also, we know from our cone, that the longer the shot goes the more it is likely to stray offline. That presents us with a widening cone approaching a narrowing fairway.

Again, depending on your tolerance for risk and reward, also on the side of your bias to the cone, you need to decide for yourself if you want to take on the challenge. For example; the following fairway is the fifth hole at Augusta National Golf Club, home of the Masters Championship every spring. It is a demanding and long par four which always averages as one of the most difficult for the week.

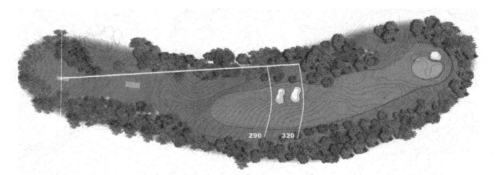

Above is a map of the hole and below is what the view looks like from down on the tee.

The bunkers you see on the left of the fairway could almost be regarded as a penalty shot. They are very deep and sit a considerable way below the level of the fairway and green, getting to the green from here is seldom done. As you can clearly see, the distance of the first bunker starts at 290 yards from the championship tees and the second bunker finishes at 320 yards, a perfect distance to catch a professional's driver. The dilemma here though is you do not want to leave yourself too far back as the second shot becomes very long indeed. If we overlay a standard cone with a dispersion of twenty percent over the fairway, we can see that those bunkers eat into the area of a driver distance. The fairway itself is actually very wide at 60 yards across. However, the bunkers take up exactly half of the width at the 300-yard mark, leaving only 30 yards of room.

A player who naturally starts the ball right and curves it back to the left is going to have the bias of their cone on the right-hand side. They would have probability on their side and may fancy taking the risk of getting that extra distance. This is what the commentator means when they say the hole fits their eye. The ball is going to start its flight in the safe area to the right and work its way back to the centre. In the rare case that the curve is overdone, they may find themselves in the bunker, but in general the risk was worth taking to leave a shorter shot to the green.

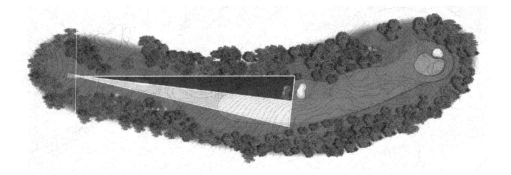

However, the player who naturally starts the ball left and curves it right is going to have a much tougher time on this hole. The bias of their cone is on the left side which brings the bunkers into play the majority of the time. If they try to compensate by aiming further right, the slippage area on the right of the cone starts to get into deep trouble too. This player may have to take defensive action here and reduce the distance by hitting a three-wood. By choosing the three-wood they can still make a positive swing with no fear of reaching the bunkers and an almost guaranteed possibility of finishing on the fairway, although resulting in a longer second shot to the green.

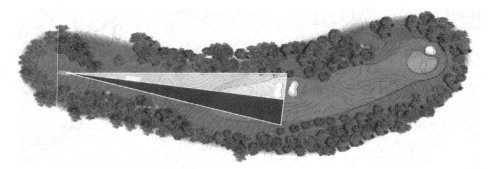

Augusta is known as a drawer's course (for right-handed golfers) as the majority of the holes set up this way. However, all courses are designed differently, most try to keep a balance between the two. You will find some holes that suit your style of shot and others which do not.

Exercise 2 - Preparing your drives

A wise golfer will not leave these decisions to the last minute. There are enough things to keep you occupied during a round of golf, especially when adjusting for weather conditions such as wind and rain. All of the drives would be planned out in advance. By doing the homework beforehand you will get a few advantages.

Firstly, less stress of having to calculate the distances during the round. We usually don't have expert caddies that do this for us like those on tour. Calculating distances have to be done when approaching the green because we don't really know where we will be playing from or where the hole will be cut. However, from the tee we do, it rarely changes from day to day. Having everything prepared allows us to relax, make adjustments if necessary and think more about following our process pre-swing.

Secondly, we don't want to focus on trouble areas before the shot. Your body tends to follow that which you are predominantly focused on. If a large amount of time is given to the danger that lurks, our subconscious might get confused about where it is we want to go. Doing this *dirty work* at home and in advance allows you to notice the danger in a safe environment so that when you get to the tee your only focus is where you want the ball to go.

Thirdly, by preparing in advance the shot that you want to hit, you are creating memories that can be recalled. No different to the visualisation exercises from before. You are reassuring yourself that you have made the correct decision amongst all the options available and pictured in advance the shot that you are going to play. This can't fail to help your mental game when on the course.

So, for this exercise take a course planner from your local course and go through each of the holes planning your wisest tee shot. If you are playing an unfamiliar golf course use Google Earth. It's free to download on to your computer and is very accurate. There is a ruler option on the menu bar which can be changed to yards or meters, whichever you normally use. By clicking on the tee and stretching the line away you can measure the distance along the ground and also measure the width of the landing area.

1) Notice danger areas around the driving area. Danger areas are those which will directly incur a penalty. Is the safer side to the left or right?
2) Does the fairway narrow at your driving distance. If it does, by how much?

3) Does your natural shape of shot and bias on the cone aim towards the trouble? If that side is free from too much punishment you can consider going for the maximum distance and hitting a driver. If your shot is likely to finish in trouble, plan to use a shorter club and accept that you'll have to build a strategy from there instead.

This is a process that I have used consistently in the past when travelling long distances to play a tournament. You may only get one practice round the day before it starts, so going prepared helps to ease the stress prior to starting. I would chart the golf course using Google Earth, visit the club's website and look at the hole by hole guide that most have. Using photographs of the hole, I could then picture roughly what it looked like and what type of shot it would require off the tee. Using the visualisation techniques from before, I could imagine playing the hole perfectly, all before even setting one foot on the property. It gives you a sense of calm, like you've played there before and know what to expect.

So, to complete this exercise, chart all eighteen holes of your local course or a course you will be playing soon. Look at the dangers and different options you have off each tee and make a decision on what you will do now. Then take that plan to the course and use it. You can adjust it if weather conditions are abnormal. For example; if a hole you had planned to hit three-wood off is playing directly into the wind, you may be able to use a driver and still avoid reaching any trouble. Like everything in golf, we must be flexible and adapt, but the plan you have created will form the basis of your strategy.

CONE THEORY: APPROACHING THE GREEN

When approaching the green, we can still plan as much in advance as possible, although we can only roughly predict the distance. We also don't know where the flag will be located until that day. Similar to the drive, we can chart any danger areas such as water or fierce bunkers in advance and imagine scenarios if the hole is cut in different positions. This part of the game is where we have to make quick and wise decisions on the go. But before we delve into this, let's look a quick scenario.

Let's take the example of two players of similar ability, both of whom hit a left to right fade which occasionally turns into a slice but always starts left of the target. Player A is Willy the Wise and Player B is Harry the Hacker.

They have both hit good drives off the first tee and have a good feeling about the upcoming round, it's always nice to get that first tee shot away. The green on this par four is generously wide but danger lurks. There is a stream that runs down the left side about 10 yards from the edge of the green, it doesn't look threatening but a bad bounce off the left edge could easily result in a penalty drop. Back right of the green there are some bunkers as well as a big, but fairly flat one short and right. The flag today is on the left side of the green, not tight, roughly five steps from the edge.

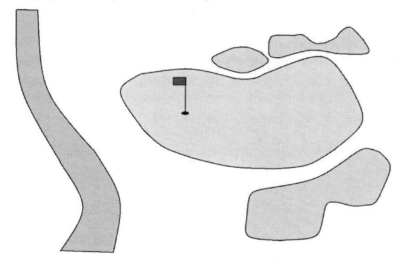

They are standing down the fairway with a mid-iron in their hands and Willy is the first to play. Harry watches as Willy's ball takes off straight at the flag. It lands over the hole, takes a skip or two and stops, setting up a nice birdie putt.

"Great shot," says Harry, "perfect". He meant it sincerely, but his competitive juices start flowing just a little bit. Harry and Willy always have a side bet going and Harry doesn't want to go behind this early in the round. Harry takes aim at the flag too, strikes it well and holds his finish. The ball starts left as it usually does however it's not curving back. He clenches his teeth and watches as the ball lands a little past the hole but in the area between the green and the water. It bounces left slightly and rolls into the stream. He can't believe it. In his mind he struck the shot perfect, it didn't deserve a watery fate. He's going to be one down for sure now.

"Bad luck Harry," shouts Willy, "you struck it great, tough break." But Willy knows it wasn't his technique that was at fault, it was his strategy.

What Harry doesn't know is that Willy didn't hit a perfect shot. In fact, he wasn't even aiming at the flag. He pulled the shot left, no different to Harry, but he wasn't going to tell him that.

Willy, being the wise golfer he is, had calculated that the flag was five steps from the edge of the green and potential trouble on the left side. He knows that from one hundred and fifty yards out he has fifteen yards of margin each side. As well as this, there is a high probability that his shot will finish in the left half of his cone. Therefore, he picked a spot aiming towards the bunker at the back centre of the green. With the club he used he knew he couldn't reach it, so it allowed him to make a nice positive swing. If the ball curved back like it usually does, it would be in the centre of the green. If it curved too much, a slice, there was plenty of room right. With a slice it may have lost a little distance, bringing the bunker at the front right into play, but that was the lesser of the evils around the green. In the end he struck the shot great, just like Harry and it didn't curve like normal. It stayed ten yards left, which is where the hole was located, looking like a fantastic shot from where Harry was standing.

When watching golf on the television we are bombarded with great shots landing close to the flag. It's important to remember though, that these are highlights, chosen to be aired by the broadcaster, of the best players in the world. I can promise you that, at least half of these shots were not aimed intentionally at the flag and that's not to mention all the boring shots cut from reaching your screen, which finished in the centre or *fat part* of the green.

Flags are rarely cut in the centre of greens. There are two reasons from this. Firstly, especially during competition rounds, they are placed in difficult tight corners of the green to entice the Harry of this world to take on risks they probably shouldn't. Secondly, maintenance teams like to preserve the playing areas the best they can. By using one side of the green they concentrate the traffic on that side and conserve the other for the next day.

Willy the Wise's method of calculating a strategy doesn't have to be a long process. We can't hold up play unnecessarily while we go through every scenario in our head. The strategy he came up with forms part of his pre-shot routine, a subject which has two distinct phases (explained in the next chapter). The first of which is decision making. We usually have less than one minute to prepare and execute our shot, so leaving all of this until the moment we reach our ball is going to cause a rush. We never want to be rushing on the golf course, especially when it comes to decision making, it leads to doubt, which leads to tension and bad swings.

Exercise 3 - Charting Greens

Doing your homework and preparing these decisions in advance helps to lessen the load when it's your turn to play. If you get the chance, note in advance any danger areas around the greens, especially those which are hidden. Sometimes these areas are not visible when standing back down the fairway. Also, try to imagine what you would do if the flag was at the front, back, left or right of the green. It might be that a bunker at the back is not particularly complicated if the flag position is at the front of the green. However, if the flag is located at the back and the green slopes downhill from the bunker, this is a place you definitely do not want to be. As you can see, danger areas sometimes depend on where the hole is located because an impossible chip or impossible bunker shot can be no different than a direct penalty. If you can find out this information in advance it helps reduce the workload when out on the course. This may seem like a complicated task, but I'll explain below a simple way of going about it.

If your course planner has a detailed green view and you can draw on it directly, you can use this. If not, buy a cheap flip pad and draw the basic shape of the green, any hazards and large slopes. Next, mark a big cross over any penalty areas, we want to avoid these at all cost. Then place a dot in a corner where you think a flag could be and decide if there are any areas nearby that would make life complicated. It could be any shot severely downhill, a steep slope or awkward bunker. Draw a line from the dot to this area and place another small cross. It will signify that if the flag is in this position, you should avoid this area too.

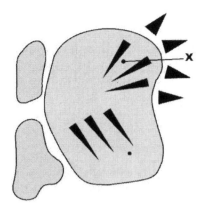

As you can see in the example, a flag on the front right of this green has no danger on the short side, it leaves a simple uphill chip. However, when the flag is on the back right, there is danger missing right despite having no bunkers. The slope is steep and once on the green it is all downhill, making this a very difficult chip indeed. With this information on hand you can then decide on course whether your cone and bias are likely to include the trouble areas.

A natural drawer of the ball, who has their bias on the right side of the cone, could take dead aim at the flag on the front right. If their shot finishes slightly right, they will have a very simple chip into the slope of the green. However, if the flag is located back right, they would need to take defensive action. Any ball finishing right risks entering the danger zone for this flag. In this situation they would be wiser aiming to the centre-left of the green to allow some margin for the bias. If the shot curves too much to the left, into the slippage area, the bunker is not a bad place to be.

A natural fader of the ball, who has their bias on the left side of the cone would be completely the opposite. To the front flag they should aim slightly right, towards the safe area. If their shot stays in the left half of their cone it would probably finish close. Their centreline and slippage area both leave simple chips. However, the back flag could be attacked if they wish. Their bias here is in the safe part of the green and any ball curving too far right still has room to finish on the green the majority of the time.

CONTINGENCY PLANNING

Another area of prepared strategy, which is a little more advanced, is planning for contingencies. A contingency plan involves looking for a spot where you would like to play from in case you hit a bad drive and can't continue the hole as originally planned. If you find trouble on the hole and reaching the green proves impossible or too risky, where is the place that allows you to play a safe shot out of trouble and the best chance of hitting the green with the next? That way we can take big numbers out of the equation and leave yourself the best opportunity to make a par or at worst a bogey.

Decide on a distance or two that you feel particularly comfortable with, this may be a wedge from one hundred yards and a pitch from fifty yards for example. Look through the plan of the par fours and fives and check if this area is accessible and safe. Mark it with a circle, now you have a spot to play to if you do find yourself in trouble and the green isn't an option.

Designing a strategy and including all the elements of driving, greens and contingencies does take time. There is no free lunch when it comes to playing good golf, your preparation will pay its dividends. Taking the time to plan a good round, I believe, is just as important and enjoyable as playing itself. People will spend hours watching instructional videos or reading magazines but rarely dedicate time to something as important as this. Are you going to be different? Are you going to out-smart the competition? Are you willing to put in the effort to saving vital strokes which could be the difference between winning and losing?

Chapter 8: Preparation and Energy

"Luck is a matter of preparation meeting opportunity" -
Lucius Annaeus Seneca

INTRODUCTION

In my opinion preparation is where all of the elements of physical golf and psychological golf come together and determines the success that you deserve. Seneca two-thousand years ago identified that opportunities will be missed if you are not prepared for them. Gary Player famously stated after holing out a bunker shot that the more he practiced the luckier he became. Preparation is the homework, the boring, un-sexy stuff that goes on behind the scenes.

During a dinner one evening with Ryder Cup player Stephen Gallagher, I asked about the work ethics of himself and his peers, especially how it had changed after the revolution caused by Tiger at the turn of the millennia. He compared it to a theatre production. It's almost impossible to comprehend the number of hours and effort that goes into a two-hour show which is what you see as the end result. Most golf fans might watch a few hours on a Sunday evening when things get interesting and mistakenly think that we have natural talent. The truth is talent will only get you so far, it's what you do after which determines if you're going to make it.

YOU CAN'T DEFINE PREPARED

I started this chapter stating that preparation was the accumulation of all the elements that determine success. Preparation though, is very hard to define by itself. It is best described as a *feeling of readiness* and this can be different for every player. A one size fits all rarely works for anything in golf, each player has to find their own method through help, guidance and experimentation.

There are players such as Bruce Lietzke, who played on the PGA tour for almost twenty years, winning twice and then winning multiple times on the senior Champions tour including a major, the U.S. Senior open. The golfing world sadly lost him in 2018 after fighting brain cancer. Bruce rarely ever practiced; in fact, he was known for literally unzipping his flight bag on the first tee. Some say that playing golf was just a job for him, his real passion was fishing, hunting and collecting classic sports cars.

However, what's interesting is Bruce describes in his own words how he played his best golf after having ten weeks off. He says it was possible because he hadn't changed his swing since 1974. That was thirty-seven years without a swing thought! What an amazing feeling that must be.

It's important to note here with caution, that's what worked for Bruce. He obviously practiced early in his career to get to the standard of a professional golfer. He most certainly hit some putts at each tournament also, to get a feel for the speed of the greens. But his preparation was to come to a tournament fresh and use his energy playing golf, not trying to perfect it.

Other players practice obsessively. Vijay Singh, the golfer from Fiji who became world number one during his career and winning multiple major championships, is still regarded as the most devoted "range rat" in the game. Where you or I take a bucket of balls to the range, he takes a trash bin. Caddies recall eight-hour practice sessions where lunch was bought out to them so not to waste any time, and that was an off week. Tournament weeks would increase to two hours before play, four on the course and practice after until light permitted, totalling usually ten to twelve hours. He had even been spotted Christmas morning hitting balls, that's dedication for you. However, this worked for Vijay, it wouldn't have worked for Bruce.

The above two examples are extremes but highlight how each player feels prepared in different ways. Some can't hit the first tee shot without practicing that precise shot one hundred times the day before, others don't feel the necessity to do so, it would just complicate things and maybe install doubt rather than reduce it. Golf is such a psychological game; it usually comes down to the one who feels best standing over the ball. So, what can I recommend to you about preparation? In my experience there are a few musts. Preparation can be separated into two categories; there is shot preparation and there is round or tournament preparation. Firstly, we'll look at shot preparation, also known as the *pre-shot routine*.

PRE-SHOT ROUTINE: PHASE 1

Start preparing your strategy about fifty yards before reaching your ball. This can be hard to do if you are using a buggy, however there are small things that you can do. A wise golfer will go through the following steps.

1) Finish, or put on hold any conversations that have been started, there will be time after to continue them if you wish. You don't want to be rushing to finish a story or engaging in chit-chat at this point, it doesn't do the conversation or your golf any justice.

2) If you haven't planned the greens in advance, now is the time to notice any danger spots. These are penalty shots such as water, out-of-bounds or a particularly difficult bunker. Also, if the flag is cut close to the edge of the green, how is a chip or pitch going to be from that side? Another phrase that is commonly heard on the television is; *missing it on the short side*. Often, and especially on fast greens, missing on the wrong side and leaving very little green before the flag makes a normally simple chip a very difficult task. However, it's not always the case, if the area is relatively flat and the grass is short, sometimes it's not a bad option. *(See Strategy chapter)*

The first two steps can often be done before reaching your ball. In fact, any time we are looking for danger, it's best to do it away from your shot. Once you reach the ball, we can start looking at the shot in more detail.

3) Take a measurement to the flag using a chart, GPS or range finder device if permitted.

4) Decide if your cone for that length of shot will bring into play any of the danger areas we highlighted before. If it does, we have two options:
- a) adjust the aim so that your bias is clear of any trouble (preferably the slippage area too)

b) adjust the distance by taking more or less club to play for a fatter part of the green

5) Make adjustments for any special conditions such as: wind, hard or soft ground, sloping lies, etc.

The previous five steps will give you a good picture of what you intend to do and help to remove any doubt that you have. With a concrete plan of what the shot requires we have succeeded in following Willy's method from the previous chapter of playing smart and to your strengths without being affected by anyone else. Once this phase is complete, we can start phase two of the pre-shot routine.

PRE-SHOT ROUTINE: PHASE 2

Phase two of the pre-shot routine is very individual. No one player is alike, they all vary slightly just as their swings, tempo and style of play do. There are two main objectives that everyone is trying to achieve, no matter how they go about it. The first is to get the mind ready and focused, the second is to keep the body relaxed. A good pre-shot routine should include elements which help to attain both.

Almost every pre-shot routine in top level golf, once they are in phase two, lasts between fifteen to thirty seconds. Also, they never deviate from the time that they take. If their time is twenty seconds, it will be within a couple of seconds of that every time they play. Anything that distracts them during this period will mean starting the process again, this requires a full commitment to the shot.

Below are elements that you can include into your pre-shot routine. You don't have to use all of them, but it should include at least one mental process and one physical process.

MENTAL OPTIONS

1) Use visualisation to see the swing you are going to make. You may have seen a swing that you like on video during a lesson or watched yourself in a mirror and can picture what your swing actually looks like from someone else's view.

Using this technique, it's important to be as specific as possible. For example; if you are playing a special shot such as a low one, you can imagine a shorter swing than normal, a steeper punching attack or whatever it is you do to hit a lower flight. If you are trying to purposely shape the flight one way or another, imagine swinging across the path to create the desired effect. Try to picture what this next swing is going to look like from another's viewpoint.

2) Use visualisation to see any key points which help you make a good swing. If you are currently working on any changes in your technique, these will be any positions you are practicing at the moment. After success and building confidence in any change on the practice range, you can picture yourself making those movements in your swing, just to remind yourself of the good memories. Using this visualisation, it's not necessary to imagine the swing in its entirety, just repeat the special move a few times in your mind before approaching the ball. For example; someone who has been working on making their swing shorter because an over-swing was causing inconsistency. They have had some success on the range with a feeling of swinging only three quarters of the way back and maybe seen the change on video and liked it. They would picture that perfect top of the backswing position a few times to trigger the good memories stored in the subconscious from the practice session before.

3) Use visualisation to see the flight your ball is going to take. Picture the starting direction and trajectory of the ideal shot, how the ball will curve in the air and where it will land and stop. Here we see the importance of planning the shot correctly from the Strategy chapter. We don't want to visualise our shot flying over or towards danger areas if we can help it. This will induce doubt and tension if you are imagining that just before your shot, it's much nicer to see the ball flying towards a safe open part of the course and moving towards your target.

4) Use kinaesthetic visualisation to imagine how the swing and strike will feel. A method described best by Australian Jason Day. You may have seen him on television closing his eyes briefly whilst standing behind the ball. He explains that; after picturing clearly the shape and trajectory of his ball flight, he then tries to imagine how that would feel through his hands, specifically through impact. Are his hands going to work fast and rotate to draw the ball or are they going to feel passive and hold the clubface open to fade it. You sometimes see other players doing this too, standing with their eyes closed just moving the hands and arms imagining the feeling of holding a club and striking the perfect shot.

These above points can be used in any combination and any order. It's up to you to experiment and find something that works and feels comfortable to you.

PHYSICAL OPTIONS

Below are four more elements we see in top level golfers, however this time, they are physical movements. Like the mental elements, you don't have to include all of them but each one has a purpose.

1) Making practice swings - Practice swings come in many shapes and sizes, another example of one size not fitting all. Let's look at a few different types so you can decide what may be best for you.

The non-existent practice swing - it's true some players don't use a practice swing. You see this for the full swing and also sometimes with putting. I went through a stage playing without a practice swing for full shots. I figured that the kinaesthetic visualisation I was using created a great feeling of what I was trying to achieve and often, if I then took a practice swing it would ruin it all and my mind would start thinking of something else. This is maybe the chore of being a coach and not a full-time player. Other colleagues of mine have experienced the same phenomena. As coaches we study on a day to day basis golf techniques, usually looking for errors and ways to correct them, like an auditor would in a company's financial records. It's hard sometimes to switch off and you can find yourself analysing your own technique and trying to correct it, even when playing. As we know from all the previous chapters, this is not the mindset we want whilst out on the golf course. I bring this point up, not as an excuse for any of my bad rounds, but because I know there are many people out there who are obsessed with swing technique, even if it's not their job to be. Clearly, this is one of the reasons people get addicted to the game, it appeals to their analytical minds and they get sucked into the never-ending cycle of finding "the secret" or the next fashion, although usually just old theories repackaged and branded.

If you consider yourself one of these people, it may be worth considering playing without a practice swing. By all means, analyse, experiment and practice off the course to your heart's content, but trust it when on the links, leave the criticising and analysing until afterwards. If you are an intermediate to advanced golfer already, you know how to hit the ball, you've done it thousands of times before. Use the visualisation techniques above, imagine the perfect swing, step in and hit it. There's no need to over-complicate things, risk making a practice swing that didn't feel right and trigger the analytical bug waiting to swarm in and bite you.

The waggle practice swing - is a half-step away from not having a practice swing. It consists of a small movement, a half-swing at the most, just to get a feel for the club. I've found whilst teaching beginners on the course, this is a great way to increase coordination and confidence. All the golf clubs we use are a different length and lie angle, so our brains have to coordinate and adjust for this each time. These subtle differences can be calculated by simply making a couple of small movements trying to brush the grass with the clubhead. You can take this a step further and look for something small on the ground to make contact with. Make sure it is smaller than the ball, a dead piece of grass, small leaf or similar. Use a small waggle or half swing to try and move the object from the ground. Your brain will have to work out the length of the club, the weight of the club and lie of the clubhead in order to successfully make contact with the ground. It's great for developing hand and eye coordination which is why I use it so often with beginners.

The key practice swing - the key practice swing requires a very focused mind in order to not be distracted by other parts of the swing. With this practice swing we make the whole movement but focus only on a key area which will help us produce the intended result. It's a physical version of the kinaesthetic visualisation in the previous section. The focus can be on a key movement or exercise that you are practicing to improve your technique. If possible, you can recreate that exercise as a practice swing or come up with a similar version you can use quickly on the course. The focus can also be on the type of shot you are going to play, making shorter or longer swings to control the distance and trajectory. Also, swinging excessively across the intended line to produce side spin and curve the ball. Whatever it is that you regard as your key, it is vitally important to remain focused only on that point. If you find your mind wondering into other parts of your swing you are in danger of entering the analysis mode, a mode we want to stay away from whilst playing. So, use this practice swing with caution, if you can maintain the focus great, if not, I would recommend using one of the other options.

The dancing practice swing - on the golf course tempo and rhythm are everything. From a technical point of view, these two are curative by nature. We've all hit good shots, no matter how many flaws we have in our swing. They happen because the subconscious mind has an amazing ability to calculate and compensate complications in our swing so that it produces our desired result. To test this, while practicing try aiming away from your target but focus totally on where you want the ball to finish. Start on a short putt but in theory you can do this for any shot. Relax your hands, swing slow and smooth and watch how your body automatically makes adjustments to achieve the objective. When we lose our tempo and rhythm the subconscious struggles to make the necessary calculations and one error becomes more dominant causing an offline shot or bad strike. Keeping a nice rhythm on your practice swings is paramount to repeating it during your real swing. Make two or three swings continuously, meaning don't stop and reset. Swing back and forth keeping everything relaxed. we're not aiming or even caring about correct positions, only the nice flowing sensation of the swing. You can make two or three of these swings without worrying about losing time because there is no stopping and thinking, it's just a back and through, back and through totalling in a handful of seconds. I call it the dancing swing because, if you have ever tried to dance, positions mean very little if you are not in time with the music. The golf swing functions very similar.

There is no right and wrong way to make a practice swing and if you watch golf on the television, you'll see all of the examples above and even some others. Experiment with what works for you. Ask your teaching professional next time you have a lesson about what you should do to get the desired feeling on to the golf course. The practice swing should be consistent, but that's not to say it's static. It evolves over time like your entire game. You may find if you have been making changes to your technique, that you may need to use the key practice swing to ingrain the movement faster. After a period of adjustment and when you feel confident in the changes you can revert to one of the other methods which help to keep the mind clear of technical thoughts. Whatever you have chosen for the time being, you must do consistently. Use this method in your practice, when playing friendly games as well as in competition. If it constantly changes from one to another, you'll fail to get the advantages of comfort that a proper practice swing can offer. Remember, feeling comfortable is the whole objective of any pre-shot routine.

2) Move slow and deliberately when approaching the ball. Rushing is never good on the golf course. It requires quick jerky movements of the muscles and makes the mind uneasy. A good pre-shot routine, which is streamlined (doesn't take too long) and consistent should lead to a feeling of being relaxed. We don't want to upset this by rushing at the last second. Sometimes it's difficult, for example if people are waiting behind. However, there are many other ways to increase the speed of play, your pre-shot routine should not be one of them. When stepping into the ball to set your alignment and ball position, do it smoothly and precisely. Doing this keeps you relaxed and ensures the set-up is as good as it can be.

3) Have a waggle - Not everyone uses the waggle, some have big waggles, some have small waggles. The waggle is a very personal thing. Ben Hogan swears by it and dedicates a large section to it in his book *Five Lessons*. The idea of the waggle comes from two main theories. Some describe it as tracing the correct path you want the club to take, this is seen as a very pronounced waggle in players such as Jason Day and Mike Wier. They either recreate the beginning of the takeaway, moving the arms and club away together, or in Hogan's case, his wrists move forward towards the target whilst the clubhead moves back, recreating the feeling prior to impact.

Others use it to release tension in the wrists and arms. By having a waggle or two helps to loosen the muscles in the arms and hands. The very act of moving the club causes the tensing of certain muscles, once the act is over the muscles can return to a relaxed state. It's a mini version of the body relaxing exercise from chapter 2. Conscious relaxation is proceeded by conscious tension. During the waggle, as your club returns to the ball, feel a relaxing of the arms and a lightening of the grip.

4) The shuffle - Whether it's an Ernie Els butt wiggle or shifting slightly the weight back and forth from the right to left foot. The shuffle is another action we see a lot in good players and acts as a version of the waggle but for the whole body. The posture in the set-up position over the ball should be athletic, balanced and relaxed. By shuffling the hips or shifting the weight you are taking the body out of this position. Like the waggle, it requires tension in the muscles to do so, any motor movement does. Shuffling for a few seconds and then returning to a balanced position helps to release tension and return the body to a relaxed state.

THE FLOW

All of these physical elements have something in common; they keep things moving. We want the whole process to keep flowing. Any stationary periods allow room for unwanted thoughts and tension to creep in.

However, you choose to go about your pre-shot routine, whichever elements you decide to include, it is important that it becomes consistent with every shot. You may develop a different routine for short shots or putting, that's okay, as long as you repeat it all the time. A good pre-shot routine should make you feel comfortable no matter what the situation. From the moment it begins you are on autopilot, just following the same steps you have taken numerous times before. It helps keep us in our comfort zone, despite what is happening around us.

My first experience in learning this was when I was a very young junior. I was watching the final of our junior match play tournament at the club I grew up at in South-East England. They were two of the older juniors at the club and had played their way through three knockout rounds during the weekend. It was Sunday afternoon and the light was fading across the old links by the seaside. I can't remember clearly the build-up to the moment because I was so young, but they had finished level after the round and preceded down the first in a sudden death playoff to decide the champion junior of the year. By this time on a Sunday evening the bar was pretty busy and word got around of the spectacle forming outside. Crowds starting gathering, fuelled by an afternoon's worth of beer and wine. The two juniors found themselves in a situation they had probably not been in before.

The first was halved and the second hole was a par five, usually reachable in two for a big junior, especially downwind. One of the players, I won't mention names but we'll call him D, had hit two good shots and left a thirty-yard pitch over a bunker for his third. Meanwhile, his opponent had found trouble off the tee but had managed to just find the green with his third. D had a good chance of making a birdie and closing out the match and a long weekend of golf right here.

He took a few practice swings and stopped. He then walked up to the green and looked at the line as if he was hitting a putt. When he eventually got back to his ball, he had another couple of practice swings, went to his bag and changed his club. He returned to the ball and took at least another half dozen practice swings with this club for which seemed like an eternity. At this point my dad turned around to me and said; "I don't think this is going to end well."

D had left his natural rhythm of playing and was placing so much emphasis on this one shot. Even though he was concentrating hard on trying to get it right, I'm pretty sure he had ever taken so many practice swings over a shot in his life. All of this was building tension and now just delaying the inevitable. Which of course happened. The simple pitch shot was hit thin, went scooting through the back of the green almost on to a road, from where he failed to get up and down and lost the hole to a par.

The pre-shot routine in its entirety is best developed and practiced on the driving range. Some part of your practice session should be dedicated to playing like you are on the course and this is the perfect opportunity to see what works for you. Quality rather than quantity is important here, take your time and treat each shot the same. Have a friend time you with a stopwatch, see how consistent you can make it. This is partly how we can transfer your driving range performance over to the course, a topic that many people complain about. The big key here though is keeping the flow. We want all of these planned and practiced stages to flow naturally, so when you find yourself in a position similar to D, you can rely on it and feel as comfortable as possible.

TOURNAMENT PREPARATION AND ENERGY

As we discussed at the beginning of this chapter, *feeling ready* is achieved by different means by different players. Tournament preparation and energy are closely linked. For some players, extreme amounts of preparation do not affect their energy levels, like Vijay Singh. For others, like Bruce Lietzke, too much preparation can cause fatigue and unnecessary complications. Some players such as Phil Mickleson are known to take Wednesday off before the tournament starts on Thursday. He arrives at the venue on Monday or Tuesday, depending on travel, and does his homework on the golf course. However, the day before the event he takes off to spend time with his family and relax. It helps keep a balance in his life and leaves him with plenty of energy for when it matters, Thursday morning.

There are a few elements which contribute to the *feeling of readiness* we are looking for. If we can include these into the build-up to a competitive round we can be physically and psychologically peaking at the right time.

Design a Strategy - Having a game plan for the day helps us stay in the comfort zone. In reality we don't know what to expect, anything can happen, but having a plan keeps our mind at rest and stops us from making rash, stupid decisions. Forming a plan starts with knowing the golf course. If it's a local course you usually play it should be no problem, however if you are travelling away you may have to look at course maps like what was suggested in the previous chapter.

Start by deciding your driving strategy on all the par fours and par fives. Decide which holes suit you and want to attack, also the holes which will require you to play more defensive. Mark this down on the course guide or a notepad for easy reference, or commit it to memory if you can. Have a strategy for each green as described in the previous chapter and plan for contingencies. Doing this will give you a sense of déjà-vu when confronted with the situation on the course.

Focused Practice - Focused practice means tailoring your practice sessions leading up to an event to suit the course you are playing. If you are a player who practices heavily, a large proportion of your practice time should be dedicated to a variable and competitive style of practice. Minimise all technical practice as much as possible. For example; if you have been making changes in your swing, assign ten to twenty percent of your time to the exercises you have been practicing. Better still, don't include it at all. Focus instead on controlling the flight of the ball and making it as consistent as possible.

If the course you are going to play requires a certain type of shot, now is a good time to practice it. On a seaside links course, you may want to practice hitting the ball lower. If the course is short, you should get your wedges as precise as possible. If you plan on hitting driver off every tee, dedicate more time to striking solid drives.

If you are a Bruce Lietzke type and prefer not hitting too many balls on the range, now is a good time to focus on short game. Give extra time to chipping and putting and make sure you have a good touch in the hands. Keep the practice as variable as possible, play games against a friend or set challenges for yourself that mimic the real game. We want to be in a competitive frame of mind at this stage, dependent much more on the result than we would be when practicing technique.

Warm Up - The warm up is, in my opinion, the greatest difference between top level golfers and the average player who doesn't improve. With very few exceptions, top golfers will never arrive on the first tee without warming up first. Most amateurs may arrive at the course early...to have a coffee.

Golf is a physical game, however important the psychological aspect is, it still requires the movement and coordination of all the muscles in the body. The *feeling of readiness* we are looking for doesn't come with a stiff back and the first shot of the day being arguably the most important. The first shot of the day should be in a non-threatening environment, i.e. the practice ground and it should be with a body that's already stretched and warmed up.

A professional tour player will generally arrive at the course an hour and a half before their round allowing time to check their equipment, put their golf shoes on, check in for their round and get to the practice range. Their first shots may be a few putts or, if they go to the range first, a handful of short pitch shots. Working up to mid-iron shots and then longer shots, they will concentrate on rhythm and any specialist shots they might require for the day. Usually they will finish with the club and type of shot they intend to hit off the first tee, before heading off to hit a few chips or return to the putting green. The whole routine is as consistent as possible and finishes ten minutes before their start leaving time to get to the first tee.

Their day usually starts before arriving at the golf club though. A physical warm up routine precedes the golf, either at the hotel or in the fitness trailer that accompanies the tour. They will arrive at the venue with a body ready for action, well alimented and already physically warmed up.

Realistically, you may not have the time or facilities that the top players have but there is no excuse to arrive at the first tee cold and unprepared. Almost all golf courses have a putting green, short game area, practice range or at least some nets to hit balls into. Try to dedicate at least ten minutes to each area if you have the facility available.

In the putting area, aim to get a feel for the speed and knock in a dozen or so short putts. Make sure the putts are short enough to make the majority of them, hearing the ball fall into the hole gives you a surprising amount of confidence before the round. In the short game area, start with a few chip and run shots to different targets, follow this with some higher pitch shots and some from the bunker if possible. On the range or in the net, make swings with a short iron to warm up. Starting with short irons helps to establish a good rhythm and tempo because with these clubs there is less tendency to seek length and hit hard. Try to finish by striking a nice shot with the club you'll use from the first tee.

In just thirty minutes you will have not only have warmed up your body for golf but also improved that all important coordination between your eyes, hands and club. The first shot of the day will have been in an area of no importance so it doesn't matter whether it was good or bad. We tend to remember the last thing we have done, if this was a putt falling in the hole, a well struck pitch or a crushing drive, we can't fail to arrive at the first tee in a positive frame of mind.

STAYING IN THE COMFORT ZONE

Feeling prepared for a round of golf requires that some homework is done in advance, however leading up to an event it is important that we stay as relaxed as possible despite the rising tension the nearer we get to our starting time. Staying within our comfort zone is impossible if we want to advance in anything we do. We have to take that leap of faith into the unknown in order to acquire the experience and knowledge we don't yet have. This is unavoidable and a major reason why many people don't attain all they are capable of in life, the unknown can be a scary place. Once we get over this instinctive response though, our comfort zone expands and now includes the once unknown. Having said that, when approaching the unknown we can trick ourselves into feeling a sense of comfort, even when stepping outside. Here are some tricks you can use that help to keep you feeling in a place of familiarity.

Location familiarity - As suggested previously in the book, getting familiar with the course before you arrive helps settle the mind. Not just making a strategy of the golf course, but finding out where the various facilities are such as toilets, pro-shop, practice areas, etc. Knowing these locations in advance reduces unnecessary stress in having to find them, especially before the round when there are more important things to worry about.

Equipment familiarity - Other small details, that might seem silly but put together make a difference, are making familiar locations for everything involved with your equipment. If you don't already, always use the same pockets in your bag for keeping balls, tees, your glove, etc. separate. Have half a dozen balls already prepared with your personal mark on them, plenty of tees, a pitchfork and your lucky ball-marker ready. It may seem trivial, but travel light. Empty your pockets of anything you don't need, you don't want change jingling around or your mobile phone vibrating at the top of your backswing. Not having to find stuff and having it all readily accessible in the usual place helps keep us in our comfort zone.

Auditory familiarity - It's worth noting here a technique that many top players use which never gets a mention outside of the ropes. When travelling to the course they listen to the same song, sometimes even whilst warming up with headphones on. Everybody has a favourite song, one which you know all the words to. A song that reminds you of a good memory or induces a certain feeling. Note here though, that the song should be calm and relaxing. I love rock, but playing heavy metal on the way to a golf event generates the wrong vibrations. Find a song that has a slow tempo and inspirational words. Make this your auditory warm up whilst travelling, it will keep you feeling at home even if you are far from it.

Afterword: Being Practical

I admit, there are over thirty different exercises and methods you can put into practice by the time you reach these final pages. That adds up to a great deal of time dedicated to improving at a game. Granted, some of the exercises you would have done whilst reading the chapter, but there remains many other techniques for the golf course or practice ground. It is not expected that you do all of them; they are just ideas to get you focusing in the right place for improvement.

Being practical means using this book as intended, a workbook, not a novel. I'm not trying to present any revolutionary, groundbreaking ideas. Believe me, by now the mental game of golf, and sports in general, is saturated with these types of books. What inspired me to write this one is a desire to simplify all of the information out there and create a structure to it all. I wanted to use my experiences to highlight what works, part through instruction, part through stories of myself and others.

Practical is something different for every player. A weekend golfer who would like to lower their handicap but has a full-time job and family, is not going to be able to dedicate a large amount of time. It would be wise to identify the most important aspect during the self-analysis chapter and concentrate on one or two ideas from that area. A young talented golfer with time on their hands should be able to do much more. If they have dreams of playing golf at a high level, or even as a profession, they would want to make sure there are no weak areas in their psychology. Golf has a way of finding and exploiting them.

Coaching has to adapt to the person, whether it is swing technique or mental game, everyone is unique. However, whereas your swing is on display to anyone that cares to watch it, your inner thoughts are not. So, when coaching psychology, it is best that it remains private, hence the structure of this book. I've found over the years that golfers are quick to criticise aspects of their technique, probably the ego trying to satisfy itself again, but when it comes to a weakness of mind they are unwilling to admit it. They think a golf technique lesson will solve everything when sometimes the fault is inside. It takes a brave person, or a lot of trust and intimacy, to tell others you have fear, low confidence or a poor self-image. Using a self-help book avoids the need to tell others and expose yourself. Writing your true feelings down on a piece of paper can be kept completely safe and private, thus you can be as honest about yourself as you can. Only then, can you truly improve something.

Without getting too philosophical, the world would be a better place if more people took the time to do this. But let's start with the golf course, maybe we can start a trend.

Appendix

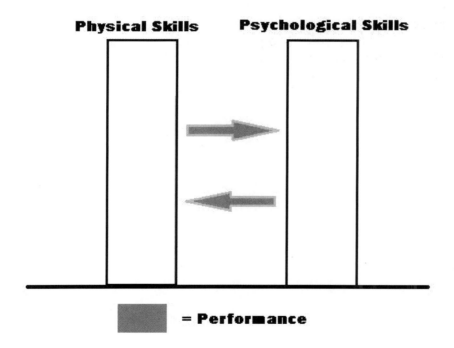

About the Author

Dean Symonds grew up in competitive golf. Ever since picking up a club at two years old, he progressed through all county ranks in England before leaving to live abroad. There he continued to qualify with the PGA of Britain and golf club management, but remains an active coach. He started writing locally developing a Practical Practice series of articles with the aim of staying away from generic topics and encouraging readers to experiment to learn. With positive feedback from these and fifteen years of coaching experience at all levels he decided to engage in his first full length feature delving into the subject of psychology, always remaining true to his philosophy of individuality in everything we do.

Printed in Great Britain
by Amazon